make!

Cath Kidston

make!

Over 40 Fantastic Projects with 16 Exclusive Designs

Cath Kidston

PHOTOGRAPHY BY PIA TRYDE

St. Martin's Griffin

New York

MAKE! Text copyright © 2008 by Cath Kidston.
Design templates and projects © 2008 by Cath Kidston.
Photography copyright © 2008 by Pia Tryde.
Design and layout copyright © 2008 by Quadrille Publishing Limited. All rights reserved.

Printed in China.

Contents

Introduction

Sewing and other crafts have had an amazing revival in the last few years. With so much mass-produced merchandise available now, people are turning away from the chain stores and toward traditional craft techniques to create unique pieces. We're tired of our clothes and our homes looking like everyone else's. And it's fantastic to see this movement spreading all across the country.

It can cost a lot to keep up with changing fashions, but the projects in this book are made using the thrifty crafts of appliqué and embroidery, which require no expensive equipment or materials; in fact, most make use of old scraps of material you might already have. Each project is in itself a joy to make, and, once you have finished, you have the added pleasure of having created something precious and completely personal to you.

Each of the 48 projects in the following chapters uses one of the 16 design templates I have included in the back of the book. All your favorites are there—the cowboy, the sailboat, an assortment of florals, and, of course, Stanley my naughty terrier—plus a few more that I have created especially for you. Every project is fully explained with step-by-step instructions, along with handy hints and suggestions to help you on your way.

I have to admit that my own sewing skills are fairly basic, so the projects here are all easily achievable—with a little patience! From the very simple to the more complicated, each project is based on the same techniques, which are outlined at the beginning of the book. Why not start off with a straightforward appliquéd T-shirt (see page 88) or the egg cozies (see page 34), before turning your hand to the more advanced cowboy skirt (see page 82) or alphabet pillow (see page 104). Each project has been given a skill level, rated from one to three, so you can easily identify which will suit your experience.

Ever since I was a little girl I have loved old printed fabrics, in fact the concept for my business was to take these wonderful vintage prints and place them in a practical modern setting. *Make!* is a continuation of this idea. What could be more satisfying than taking an original fabric design and using it to update an old skirt? And just because your bag will carry your groceries home from the stores, there's no reason why it can't be covered in flowers or brightly colored dots!

These are, of course, just starting points. At the back of the book, I have included a few extra ideas for how you can use the templates, but the fun will be in adapting the designs yourself and creating your own designs. I hope you have just as much fun with these projects as I have had putting together this book.

Cath Kidson

Techniques

This section sets out the basic techniques you will need to re-create all the items in the book—some are very simple, others a little more ambitious, so there should be something for all ages and skills! Check out our handy workbasket suggestions as well, so that once you get started you'll have everything you need.

Workbasket

WORKBASKET AND FABRICS

One of the best things about appliqué and embroidery is that neither technique requires expensive or specialized equipment—many of the items listed here may already be in your workbasket. If you don't already have a ragbag, crammed full of scraps, remnants, and fabric salvaged from worn-out clothing, now's the time to start collecting!

SEWING WORKBASKET

• Needles

A mixed packet will contain medium-length "sharps" for general sewing; shorter quilting needles for finer work; and crewel (embroidery) needles with long eyes. Triangular-pointed leather needles pierce hide without damage. Keep needles safe in a felt-leaved book. (See page 122 to make your own.)

• Thimble

This may seem a little old-fashioned but it's an essential tool. You need to protect your fingers if you are going to do a lot of sewing. Thimbles come in different sizes: choose one that fits snugly but not tightly on your index finger.

• Pins

Choose longer ones with colored heads that can be spotted easily on thicker fabrics. Store them in a pincushion.

• Scissors

You'll need two pairs: small embroidery scissors with narrow, pointed blades for cutting out intricate curves and clipping threads; and a general all-purpose pair for larger appliqué shapes, paper, and fabrics.

• Sewing thread

You will require several colors for each project, to match the fabrics that you use. You could buy lots of spools, but a good solution is to get a thread braid, which is woven from many different sewing threads in ready-to-use lengths.

• Marking tools

You will need to draw in temporary guidelines for embroidery. Use a chalk pencil to show up on dark fabrics, like denim, and a dressmaker's disappearing-ink pen for lighter backgrounds. These helpful fiber-tips have a light-sensitive pigment that disappears in a few days.

• Pencil

You'll also need an ordinary drawing pencil for tracing the template outlines onto paper-backed fusible adhesive web when you are working iron-on appliqué. Keep a sharpener at hand, so that your lines will always be precise.

FUSIBLE ADHESIVE WEB AND IRON-ON INTERFACING

Two innovative products—available from notions departments and craft stores—that make traditional needlecrafts easier. Fusible adhesive web consists of a fine layer of heat-sensitive glue attached to a paper backing. Use it to trace, cut out, and fuse on appliqué shapes in one smooth process. (Always make sure that you iron this adhesive to the reverse side of patterned fabrics.) Lightweight nonwoven iron-on interfacing is designed for dressmaking, but I've used it to transfer embroidery templates onto their background.

FABRICS

Like its sister patchwork, working appliqué is an ecological way of recycling old materials. The project instructions give the minimum amount needed if you are buying new fabric, but it's always useful to have some spare. Most of the projects use felt or cotton fabrics, but plastic-coated fabric, tweed, fleece, and leather have their own distinctive qualities.

• Felt

Felt is easy to handle as it doesn't have a "wrong" side and, because it's nonwoven, it cannot fray. Try to get all-wool felt rather than children's craft felt, which is made from synthetic fibers. Felt does not launder well, so use it for accessories or garments that will be dry-cleaned or cold hand-washed.

• Cotton and linen

Wash and iron fabrics and garments before starting work. This will remove any dressing from new cloth; freshen up old materials; and ensure your finished projects will not shrink.

YOUR EMBROIDERED AND APPLIQUÉD PROJECTS REQUIRE SPECIAL AFTERCARE. WASH THEM GENTLY IN COLD WATER WITH A GENTLE LIQUID SOAP OR SOAPFLAKES AND DRY FLAT. MORE ROBUST ARTICLES—TOWELS AND SHEETS—CAN BE MACHINE-WASHED ON A GENTLE CYCLE, BUT THEY SHOULD NOT BE TUMBLE-DRIED.

How to Appliqué

All the appliqué projects in the book are created in the same way—by cutting out fabric shapes and fixing them onto a garment or accessory. If some of them appear to be more complicated than others, that's simply because they consist of several layers of fabric, or many motifs. Once you've learned the basic technique, you can create any of the designs with ease (and a little patience!).

WORKING WITH THE TEMPLATES

The template section, which starts on page 144 onward, features two versions of each design. One is a full-color illustration and the other is a technical working diagram, which is a mirror image of the first. This is because with iron-on appliqué the design is traced onto the paper side of the fusible adhesive web, which is then fused to the wrong side of the fabric. This process requires the template to be reversed so that when the motifs are fixed in place, they will be the right way around.

Some of the outlines have been reworked to show how the various elements will be built up to create the final design. Extra fabric has been allowed on some of the shapes: this is represented by dotted lines. You'll also see that some of the fine details have been simplified to make the originals suitable for appliqué.

Many of the templates are used at their actual size, but some will need to be adjusted using a photocopier. A suggested percentage increase or reduction is given in the steps for the individual projects, but you may wish to alter the proportions to suit your own ideas and garment sizes.

1 Trace your motifs from the book, or from a photocopy, onto the paper side of the fusible adhesive web. Leave about a ½-inch space between the outlines.

2 Snip the individual shapes out roughly around the pencil lines: you don't have to be too precise with your cutting at this stage.

3 Place the motifs, adhesive facing downward, on the fabric and iron in place. When using printed cotton, make sure you fuse them to the reverse side.

4 Now cut out each of the motifs accurately, following the outline as closely as you can. Use small scissors with sharp blades, to give a clean edge.

5 Peel away the backing paper from each of the motifs, and turn them the right way up. You will be able to feel the rough adhesive layer on the reverse side.

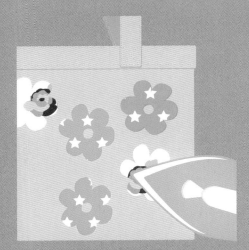

6 Position the motifs on your background and fuse them in place with a cool iron. Use a pressing rather than a sliding action, so that they do not move out of place.

If you are working with felt, always use a handkerchief or piece of muslin as a pressing cloth, so that the heat of the iron doesn't damage and distort the fabric or cause it to stick to your iron.

7 All the motifs are edged with a round of small straight stitches embroidered in a matching or contrasting thread. See how to do this on page 20.

MULTICOLORED APPLIQUÉ

The more elaborate designs—like the cowboy and the dishtowel roses—are made up from a number of different colored fabrics. The shapes are built up in layers, starting with the largest elements and finishing with the smallest details.

There are two versions of multicolored appliqué: contour appliqué and overlapping designs. With contour appliqué the layers stack up one upon the other, like the lines on a map. On overlapping designs, some of the pieces, such as leaves, are tucked beneath others.

CONTOUR DESIGNS

1 Trace each element of the reversed template onto fusible adhesive web, following any dotted lines. Cut each shape from fabric (see pages 16 and 17).

2 Peel off the papers and iron down the largest shape. Add the other layers in turn, double-checking their position against the colored version of the template at the back of the book.

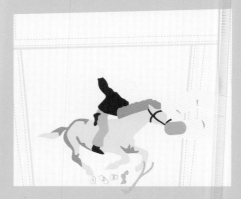

OVERLAPPING DESIGNS

1 Number the small shapes—such as these hooves—as you trace them. Write the corresponding numbers on the template, so they won't get mixed up.

2 The step-by-step instructions for each project will tell you exactly how to build up the finished design, and in which order to position the various shapes.

OTHER APPLIQUÉ TECHNIQUES

Some fabrics, including fleece, plastic-coated fabric, and leather, require a different technique, as they are thicker and cannot be ironed. To appliqué with these materials, you will first need to make a paper pattern for your motifs. The motifs are then sewn on by hand or glued onto the background.

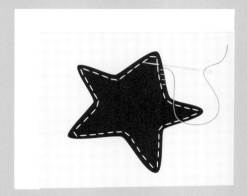

WORKING WITH FLEECE

1 To make a paper pattern, trace and cut out the template following the reversed outline, then turn it over. Pin to your fleece and cut around the edge.

2 Pin the motif to your background material and baste it in place. Remove the pins and work a round of matching straight stitches around the edge (see page 20). Remove the basting.

WORKING WITH PLASTIC-COATED FABRIC

Pencil around the reversed paper patterns on the back of the cloth and cut around the outline. Arrange the shapes and fix them down with a thin layer glue.

WORKING WITH LEATHER

It is not easy to sew through more than one layer of leather, so Stanley was redrawn in stencil style. Use a specialized leather needle to stitch down the shapes.

Basic Stitches

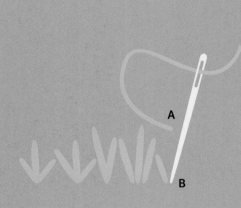

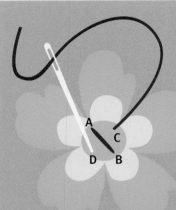

STRAIGHT STITCH

Bring your needle up at A, and take it down again at B, making a short line. Straight stitches in various lengths are used to work details, like facial features, and to "draw in" small motifs such as this grass.

STRAIGHT STITCH EDGING

Work a round of evenly sized and spaced stitches at right angles to the edge of the appliqué. When worked in matching sewing thread, this gives a subtle finish. Larger stitches in a contrasting thread create a decorative edging.

CROSS-STITCH

Work two overlapping straight stitches to form a cross. Work the first stitch from A to B and the second, at a right angle, from C to D. Individual crosses are used as feature stitches or as a decorative way of anchoring tiny appliqué pieces.

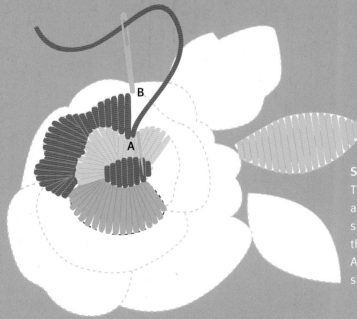

SATIN STITCH

The smooth, shiny finish produced by a row of straight stitches lying side-by-side gives this stitch its name. Work all the stitches in the same direction, from A to B and vary their lengths to fill the shape being worked.

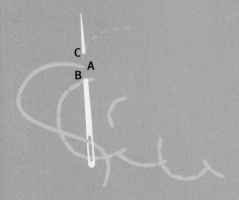

BACKSTITCH

Start with a straight stitch, worked backward from A to B, then bring the needle up at C, equidistant from B. Make another stitch back to A, and continue in the same way to the end to make a solid line of stitches.

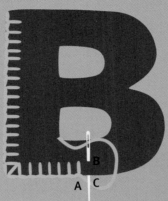

BLANKET STITCH

A traditional finish for wool blankets, this stitch is used to anchor appliqué or to join two pieces of felt. Start at A, then take the needle down at B and up again, directly below, at C. Pull it through over the thread and repeat to the end.

CHAIN STITCH

This looped stitch produces a wide line suitable for both straight lines and curves. Start at A and loop the thread from left to right. Take the needle back down at A and bring the tip up at B. Pull the needle through over the thread. Repeat this action, starting the next stitch at B.

LAZY DAISY STITCH

These are single chain stitches, where the loop is anchored with a small straight stitch. They can be worked around a central point to make sweet flower motifs. The roses on the cottage teapot cozy are made this way.

How to Embroider

HOW TO EMBROIDER

Although the approach to embroidery in this book is very informal, it's worth bearing the following points in mind as you work. You will be investing time and skill in the projects, and it's not difficult to achieve a professional finish.

WORKING WITH EMBROIDERY THREAD

Six-strand cotton embroidery floss was used for the embroidery in this book. It comes in looped skeins, held together by two paper bands. To avoid tangles, grasp one band with one hand and gently pull the loose thread out from the other end.

CHOOSING A NEEDLE

For embroidery floss, choose a crewel (embroidery) needle. This type of needle has a long eye that can accommodate all six strands of strands of the embroidery floss and pass easily through the fabric. If you are using sewing thread, you'll need a finer needle with a smaller eye (a "sharp").

STARTING AND FINISHING

Begin by knotting the end of the thread. If you are working a single line of stitches, pull the needle up through the fabric from the wrong side. For an embroidered design, you need to avoid bumpy knots, so take the needle down on the right side, ¾ inch from the area to be worked. Your stitches will anchor the surplus thread and you can clip off the knot when you have finished. Start the next length of thread by slipping the needle under the back of the existing stitches, leaving a short tail, and securing the thread with a backstitch. Finish off in the same way.

THREADING YOUR NEEDLE

Fold one end of the thread over your needle and hold the loop between finger and thumb. Slide the eye downward over the loop, then pull the loop through the eye. Work with a 18-inch length of thread: any longer and it may fray as you sew.

EMBROIDERING ONTO APPLIQUÉ

Embroidery is useful for the smallest elements of a design, such as the masts on these yachts. Here, a row of blue chain stitch, worked onto the T-shirt, reproduces the cloud outline as shown on the original design.

EMBROIDERING OVER INTERFACING

This is a great technique for working on stretchy jersey or knitted garments, such as T-shirts or socks, where the fabric has a lot of "give." The layer of lightweight nonwoven iron-on fusible interfacing stabilizes the background so that the stitches don't distort the fabric. (Remember to trace onto the smooth, nonadhesive side of the interfacing.)

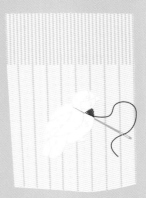

1 The outline motif should match the colored template, so reverse it on a photocopier if necessary. Trace it onto the interfacing with a disappearing-ink pen and cut out carefully. Keep track of the colors by numbering each area on the main template and the interfacing.

2 Fuse the motif onto the background, using an iron and a pressing cloth to protect the surface. Fill in each area with satin stitch, worked in the appropriate color thread—it's just as easy as painting by numbers!

TRANSFERRING OUTLINES

If you have a steady hand, you can draw embroidery guidelines directly onto the background fabric. Use a disappearing-ink pen for most fabrics and a chalk pencil on the very darkest backgrounds. Most of us, however, need a little help.

1 Cut the required shape from a photocopy of the reversed outline template. Turn it over and fit it into the appliqué design, like the last piece of the jigsaw. Draw around the outline with a disappearing-ink pen or chalk.

2 Embroider along the line using the color and stitch type given in the step-by-step instructions. Any ink that remains visible will disappear in time.

Kitchen

Some of the very first products I made for my shop were kitchen items. You can't beat a great dishtowel to cheer the place up. Whether you want to make an instant gift like an egg cozy, or you're up for something more ambitious, like a hand-appliquéd tablecloth, I hope you will feel inspired!

Linen Dishtowels

Cath Kidston

SKILL RATING: 1

WHAT YOU WILL NEED...

- 2 linen dishtowels
- Fusible adhesive web
- Old newspapers and a sheet
- Iron
- Plain cotton fabrics: scraps of red, lime green, emerald, yellow, turquoise, dusky pink, and brown
- Sewing thread to match fabrics
- Dressmaker's disappearing-ink pen
- Embroidery floss in antique white
- Sewing workbasket (see page 15)

Transform the mundane task of drying dishes into a pleasure with these cheery dishtowels.

1 For the polka dot dishtowel, use the circles on page 156 to trace 66 circles onto fusible adhesive web, and cut them out roughly. Make a temporary ironing board by covering your work surface with newspapers, topped with a folded sheet. Iron the circles onto the various fabrics, ensuring you have a roughly equal number of each color. Now cut them out accurately and peel off the backing papers.

2 Lay a dishtowel on the "ironing board" and arrange the circles across the surface. Iron them in place and edge each one with a round of matching straight stitches (see page 20).

3 For the second dishtowel, enlarge the three flowers on page 176 by 200%. For each flower, trace the outline, inner petals, and center onto fusible adhesive web, leaving about $1/4$ inch around each shape. Roughly cut out each piece and iron fusible adhesive web onto the fabric using the colored template on page 175 as a guide. Cut out along the pencil lines.

4 Iron the largest flower to the center of one end of a towel, then add its inner petals and center. Fuse on the other two flowers on either side and anchor each layer with a round of straight stitches, using matching sewing thread (see opposite page).

5 With a disappearing-ink pen, mark the positions of the small dots around the flower centers where indicated on the template. Using antique white floss, work the dots in satin stitch (see page 20).

THE POLKA DOTS WOULD LOOK VERY DIFFERENT IF THEY WERE CUT FROM PATTERNED FABRICS. WHY NOT TRY MAKING A THIRD OR EVEN A FOURTH DISHTOWEL?

Napkins and Place Mats

This simple design is a perfect starting point for the appliqué novice!

1 You will find the reversed apple and circle outlines on page 172. Enlarge them by 235%, so that the apple is about 4¼ inches wide.

2 Using a sharp pencil, trace the apple, highlight, stalk, and circles separately onto fusible adhesive web. You will need one apple and nine circles for each napkin, and four apples and 32 circles per place mat. Cut the shapes out roughly.

3 Iron the apple and the highlight onto either red or green cotton (see opposite), the circles onto green, and the stalk onto brown. Cut each shape out around the pencil line and peel off the paper backing.

4 Fold the napkin into quarters. Place the apple across one corner at an angle, with the top edge facing inward. Tuck the stalk under the top of the apple. Place the highlight at the top right of the apple. Arrange three green circles in each of the other corners. Iron the shapes in place.

5 If you are making a place mat, position the apples the other way up, s[o] that the apple tops face outward. Arrange them so that the red and gree[n] apples lie in opposite corners. Fuse on three green circles in each corner and arrange the others along the edges of the place mat.

6 Finish off by working a round of short straight stitches around each shape (see page 20), using matching sewing thread.

Cath Kidston

SKILL RATING: 1

WHAT YOU WILL NEED...

- Linen or cotton napkins and place mats
- Fusible adhesive web
- Iron
- Plain cotton fabric for each napkin: 6" square each of red and green; scrap of brown
- Plain cotton fabric for each place mat: 6" x 12" red; 8" x 12" green; scrap of brown
- Sewing thread to match fabrics
- Sewing workbasket (see page 15)

THIS TABLE LINEN WAS A LUCKY FIND — IT ALREADY HAD A RED EDGING. BUT YOU COULD ALWAYS TRIM A PLAIN NAPKIN WITH BIAS BINDING TO MATCH.

Breakfast Tablecloth

Cath Kidston

SKILL RATING: 3

WHAT YOU WILL NEED...

- White cotton tablecloth
- Fusible adhesive web
- Iron
- Plain cotton fabric: scraps of red, navy, light stone, brown, mustard yellow, white, and sage green
- Polka dot fabric: scraps of blue and pink
- Sewing thread to match fabrics
- Sewing workbasket (see page 15)

Get your day off to a cheerful start by spreading this appliquéd tablecloth across your breakfast table.

1 Firstly, enlarge the templates on page 172: the cup, bottle, and teapot by 280%, and the two eggs by 250%.

2 To decide how many motifs you need, make several copies (half of them reversed). Cut out the individual shapes and pin them symmetrically around the hem. Remove one at a time as you fill in the space with appliqué.

3 Start with a whole egg. Trace the egg and egg cup onto fusible adhesive web. Iron the egg onto light stone cotton and the cup onto red or green. Cut out the shapes and remove the papers. Position the cup, tuck the egg under the rim, and iron in place.

4 To make the half-eaten egg, follow the dotted lines for the yellow back shell, white yolk, and front shell. Position the back shell first, then layer the yolk, front shell, and egg cup on top. Iron all the pieces in place.

5 For the teapot, start by ironing on the lid and wide stripes. Then add the narrow polka dot stripes, lapping them over the top edge of the wide ones. Next, add the spout, handle, and a dark knob.

6 On the cup and bottle motif, start with the top of the bottle, then add the two pieces of the cap, the bottom outline, and shadow. Position the saucer, tuck the saucer rim underneath, and iron in place. Position the cup and slip its base underneath. Fuse on and finish off with the dark handle.

7 Secure each motif with a round of straight stitches around the edge (see page 20), using matching sewing thread.

THIS PROJECT IS TRULY A LABOR OF LOVE. IF YOUR TIME IS LIMITED, DECORATE JUST A SINGLE CORNER, OR MAYBE THE CENTRAL PART OF YOUR TABLECLOTH.

IF YOU DON'T WANT POCKETS, SIMPLY CUT THE STRAWBERRIES WITH A FUSIBLE ADHESIVE WEB BACKING AND IRON THEM DIRECTLY ONTO THE APRON, USING A PRESSING CLOTH.

Strawberry Apron

Cath Kidston

SKILL RATING: 2

WHAT YOU WILL NEED...

- Cotton apron
- Felt: 10" x 12" each of red and dark red; 4" x 6" each of light green, dark green, and white
- Fusible adhesive web
- Iron and pressing cloth
- Sewing thread to match felts
- Sewing workbasket (see page 15)

Even the most reluctant cook will feel like a domestic goddess in this pretty apron.

1 To make the strawberry pockets, enlarge the outline on page 170 by 120%, so that it is about $7\frac{1}{2}$ inches tall (including the stem). Cut the photocopy out around the outside edge to make a paper template. Pin this onto the red felt and cut out carefully around the edge.

2 Trace the dark red shadows onto fusible adhesive web following the dotted line, cut them out roughly, and iron onto dark red felt. Always use a pressing cloth when ironing felt. Cut out accurately and position on the red strawberry. Secure with a round of red straight stitches around the edge (see page 20).

3 Make the hull and stalk from light and dark green felt and the seeds from white felt. Fuse them in place with the iron, remembering the pressing cloth. Anchor each piece with a round of straight stitches, using matching sewing thread.

4 Now make a reversed copy of the enlarged template and put the second pocket together in the same way, as a mirror image of the first.

5 Pin the pockets on the apron, making sure they are level. Secure with red straight stitches, all around the berry from $\frac{3}{4}$ inch away from the green hull on the left to $\frac{3}{4}$ inch away from the hull on the right. Make a few extra stitches at each side of the opening to reinforce it.

IF YOU ARE AN EXPERIENCED SEAMSTRESS, YOU COULD MAKE YOUR OWN APRON FROM A RECTANGLE OF PLAIN FABRIC TRIMMED WITH A GINGHAM BORDER.

Egg Cozies

Cath Kidston

SKILL RATING: 1

WHAT YOU WILL NEED...

- 2³/₄" x 3¹/₂" rectangle of paper
- Ruler
- Fusible adhesive web
- Iron and pressing cloth
- Felt: 4³/₄" x 8" pink; 4³/₄" x 6" each of red and blue; scraps of light green, dark green, white, and brown
- Embroidery floss in green, brown, antique white, red, and pink
- Sewing thread to match felts
- Sewing workbasket (see page 15)

Keep your boiled eggs warm in traditional style with a trio of adorable felt cozies.

1 First make the cozy pattern, by folding the paper in half lengthwise. Draw a curve across one top corner, cut along the line, and open out. Using this as a guide, cut two shapes—a front and a back—from red, blue, and pink felt.

2 For the red cozy, trace the largest star on page 154 onto fusible adhesive web and fuse it onto pink felt with an iron—make sure you always use a pressing cloth when working with felt. Cut around the line, peel off the paper, and fuse the star onto a red felt shape. Work straight stitches around the edge (see page 20), using green embroidery floss.

3 To make the blue cozy, enlarge the single rose on the left of page 162 by 115% and trace the elements onto adhesive web. Cut them out and fix the petals to the appropriate felt, using the photograph opposite as a guide.

4 Remove the backings and center the main rose on a blue felt cozy piece. Tuck the leaves under each side, add the petals, and iron them on. Straight stitch around each piece of felt with matching sewing thread. Embroider the center of the rose in straight stitch (page 20), using brown floss.

5 For the pink cozy, reduce the small strawberry on page 170 to 60%. Using adhesive web, make the berry from red felt, then add the hull in light and dark green. Work the seeds in straight stitches, using antique white floss.

6 To finish the cozies, pin the fronts to the matching backs. Leaving the bottom open, sew together with blanket stitch (see page 21), using green floss for the red cozy, pink for the blue, and red for the pink cozy.

PLEASE DON'T FORGET TO USE YOUR PRESSING CLOTH TO PREVENT THE FELT FROM ATTACHING ITSELF TO THE SURFACE OF YOUR IRON!

Teapot Cozy

Cath Kidston

SKILL RATING: 2

WHAT YOU WILL NEED...

- Ready-made teapot cozy
- Fusible adhesive web
- Felt: 8" square of red; 4" square each of white and dark green; scraps of light blue, yellow, and brown
- Iron and pressing cloth
- Sewing thread to match felts
- 1 small button, for the eye
- Sewing workbasket (see page 15)

Teatime isn't complete without a cozy sitting on the teapot—so I have used the red rooster from my "Breakfast" fabric to cheer up this plain polka-dot version.

1 Enlarge the rooster on page 172 by 210%, or to fit your cozy. Trace the main outline (omitting the feet, coxcomb, and wattle) onto fusible adhesive web. Cut out roughly and fuse onto red felt with an iron. Always use a pressing cloth when working with felt. Cut carefully around the pencil line. Peel off the backing paper and iron the rooster to the center of the teapot cozy.

2 The details are all made with fusible adhesive web in the same way. Draw around the outside edge of the wing and cut this shape from white felt. Iron it in place, then add the green layer on top. Next add the three white feathers and the smaller blue feathers so the bird has more of a three-dimensional look.

3 Fuse on the six white tail feathers, adding two green and two blue feathers on top. Cut the foot, coxcomb, and wattle from yellow felt and iron them in place. These three pieces butt up to the main shape, without overlapping. Add the two brown shadow pieces, which fit inside the edge of the rooster's body.

4 Secure each piece with short straight stitches (see page 20), using matching sewing thread.

5 The finishing touch, which gives real character to this design, is the eye—a small white button sewn on with dark thread.

WORK THE STRAIGHT STITCH EDGING THROUGH JUST THE TOP LAYER OF THE FABRIC, RATHER THAN TRYING TO SEW ALL THE WAY THROUGH THE THICK PADDING.

DRAW THE SCALLOPED EDGE OF THE TABLECLOTH ONTO GRAPH PAPER, TRACING AROUND A COIN OR LARGE BUTTON TO CREATE THE SHALLOW CURVES.

Framed Flowerpot

Give new life to an old picture frame with this appliqué flowerpot adapted from my "Circus Flowers" fabric.

1 To make the "tablecloth," cut two 2-inch strips of fusible adhesive web to the same width as the cream background. Iron them onto gingham: one parallel to the checks, the other at right angles. Peel off the papers.

2 Iron the first strip to the background, $3/4$ inch from the bottom. Fuse on the second strip directly above. Draw a $5/8$-inch scalloped band, of the same width, onto fusible adhesive web, cut it from red felt, and iron it in place. Remember to use a pressing cloth with felt.

3 Increase the size of the template on page 176 to fit within your frame. Trace the two parts of the flowerpot onto fusible adhesive web and cut out roughly. Press the main pot onto blue felt and the rim onto brown. Cut out and fuse onto the backing. Add six red felt dots to the pot.

4 Cut out the leaves and flowers from felt and fabric in the same way, using the picture opposite as a color guide. Peel off the backings.

5 Layer the pieces, putting the blue and yellow petals in position, then adding the pink flower with its red center to the right. Tuck the leaves under the edge of the flowers as shown and add the three red petals and the blue flower center. Press all the pieces in place.

6 Edge each shape with straight stitches (see page 20), using matching sewing thread. Embroider red blanket stitch (see page 21) around the largest flower center and the dots. Add a button to each flower center, four red beads to the yellow petals, and three diamantés to the very top.

Cath Kidston

SKILL RATING: 3

WHAT YOU WILL NEED...

- Picture frame
- Thick cream fabric to fit the frame
- Fusible adhesive web
- Iron and pressing cloth
- Cotton fabric: 12" x 18" red gingham; 4" x 6" each of plain green and blue polka dot
- Felt: 4" x 12" red; 10" square each of blue, pink, and yellow; $1\frac{1}{2}$" x 6" brown
- Sewing thread to match fabrics
- Embroidery floss in red
- 3 buttons; 4 red beads; 3 diamantés
- Sewing workbasket (see page 15)

THE GINGHAM TABLECLOTH IS SKILLFULLY CUT ON THE BIAS OF THE FABRIC TO CREATE THE ILLUSION OF PERSPECTIVE.

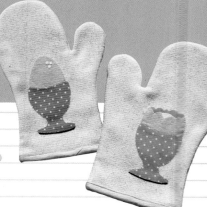

Pot Holders
and Oven Mitts

Add a touch of retro domesticity to your kitchen with these pretty, practical accessories.

1 Adjust the egg cup outlines on page 172 to fit the oven mitts: mine were enlarged by 325%. Trace the various parts of the template onto fusible adhesive web and cut out each shape roughly. Fuse the shells onto felt, using a pressing cloth, and the other shapes onto cotton fabric: white for the yolk and highlights, yellow for the inner shell, polka dots for the egg cups, and brown for the bottom rims. Cut out carefully.

2 Remove the papers and position the two egg cups on the mitts. Tuck the shells and rims under them, then add the inner shell and yolk to the half-eaten egg. Iron in place. Finish off with the three small highlights. Secure each piece with straight stitches (see page 20), using matching sewing thread.

3 Enlarge the teacup motif by 260% to fit a 8$\frac{1}{4}$-inch pot holder. Trace the cup and its rim, the saucer and its rim, and the handle onto adhesive web. Cut out roughly. Iron the cup and saucer to the back of the polka-dot and floral prints, and the other pieces to the brown fabric. Cut out carefully.

4 Peel off the backings and place the cup and saucer on the pot holder. Slip the brown rims in place, add the handle, and iron in place. To make a mirror image on the second holder, reverse the handle template and fuse it on at the other side of the cup.

5 Mark the five steam lines above the cup with a disappearing-ink pen. Chain stitch over these curves (see page 21), using brown floss.

Cath Kidston

SKILL RATING: 2

WHAT YOU WILL NEED...

- 2 oven mitts and 2 pot holders
- Fusible adhesive web
- Iron and pressing cloth
- Felt: 4" x 8" egg shell
- Plain cotton fabric: scraps of white, yellow, and brown
- Cotton fabric prints: 6" x 8" pink polka dot; 4" square of blue polka dot; 4" x 6" floral
- Sewing thread to match fabrics
- Dressmaker's disappearing-ink pen
- Embroidery floss in brown
- Sewing workbasket (see page 15)

Bedroom

I love these pillowcases covered with appliquéd dots, and it's a great way to use up scraps of fabric. You can pick up vintage bed linen at flea markets, otherwise, inexpensive basic bed linen is now very easy to find.

THE SHELL PINK THROW GIVES A VERY FEMININE LOOK TO THIS PROJECT. TO MAKE A STRONGER IMPACT, USE A DARKER BACKGROUND COLOR.

Rose Throw

Cath Kidston

SKILL RATING: 3

WHAT YOU WILL NEED...

- Pink wool throw or pashmina
- Fusible adhesive web
- Iron and pressing cloth
- Plain cotton fabric: 6" x 8" each of pink, red, light green, and dark brown
- Sewing thread to match fabrics
- Sewing workbasket (see page 15)

Transform your bedroom into a boudoir with a luxurious rose-strewn throw.

1 Trace the two main rose outlines from the template on page 164 onto the fusible adhesive web, following the dotted line at the edge of the smaller flower. Cut them out roughly. Fuse the large rose onto pink cotton and the small one onto red cotton. Cut them out accurately.

2 Peel away the papers and position the roses in the center at the end of the throw. Tuck the left edge of the red rose under the pink rose.

3 Now trace all 12 leaves onto fusible adhesive web, following the dotted and unbroken lines. Iron the adhesive side onto the green fabric.

4 For the next stage, start at the center top and work clockwise. Cut out the large double leaf, take off the paper backing, and slip the leaf behind the two roses. Position the other leaves, using the colored template on page 163 as a guide.

5 Lay a pressing cloth over the pieces to protect the throw from direct heat and fuse them on with a warm iron.

6 Sew a round of short straight stitches around each rose and leaf (see page 20), using matching sewing thread.

7 Trace all the red petals for the pink rose and iron the fusible adhesive web pieces onto red cotton. Cut out and iron on one petal at a time, double-checking the positions against the template. Make the shadows from brown cotton in the same way.

8 Add the pink petals and brown shadows to the red rose, then straight stitch around the edge of the shape in pink, red, or brown thread.

9 Appliqué a second rose motif to the other end of the throw.

I ENLARGED THE TEMPLATE JUST SLIGHTLY TO FIT MY THROW, BUT YOU COULD INCREASE THE TEMPLATE BY 200% FOR A REALLY DRAMATIC LOOK.

Hot Water Bottle Cover

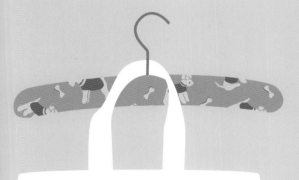

Cath Kidston

SKILL RATING: 2

WHAT YOU WILL NEED...

- Red fleece hot water bottle cover
- Sharp pencil and tracing paper
- Fleece fabric: 10" square of light stone; 4" x 8" dark stone; scrap of red fleece for collar
- Sewing thread to match fabrics
- Small button, for dog tag
- Dressmaker's disappearing-ink pen
- Embroidery floss in brown
- Sewing workbasket (see page 15)

Snuggle up to a fleecy version of Stanley!

1 Trace the Stanley outline on page 148 onto paper. Cut out his head and body, then turn the pieces over so that he faces to the right. Pin the two shapes to the light stone fleece and cut them out.

2 Position Stanley on the front of the cover, leaving a narrow gap between his head and body. Pin the shapes in place (making sure the pins don't go through the back), and baste them in position. Edge each shape with straight stitches (see page 20), using matching sewing thread.

3 Now cut out the markings on Stanley's body and leg from the paper template, turn them over and pin them onto the dark stone fleece. Cut out, then pin, baste, and sew them in place, using dark stone thread.

4 For Stanley's collar, cut a ¼-inch strip of red felt or fleece to fit across his neck. Baste it in place, then sew in place with red straight stitches. Sew a button at the center for the dog tag. Remove the basting.

5 Draw on the eyes, nose, and mouth with a dressmaker's disappearing-ink pen and embroider over the lines in satin and straight stitches, using brown floss. Cut the inner ears from scraps of dark stone fleece and sew them on with matching sewing thread.

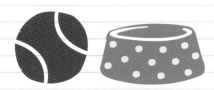

6 Use the bone on page 148 to make an appliqué motif in light stone felt and sew it to the flap with straight stitches.

YOU'LL FIND IT EASIER TO SEW THE SHAPES ONTO THE COVER IF YOU PUT ONE HAND INSIDE THE COVER TO SUPPORT THE FABRIC WHILE YOU STITCH WITH THE OTHER HAND.

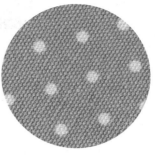

IF YOU LIKE THIS PROJECT, THEN YOU COULD TRY IT WITH A DIFFERENT MOTIF—PERHAPS THE SHOOTING STARS FOR A NIGHTTIME THEME?

Polka Dot Sheet and Pillowcase

Cath Kidston

SKILL RATING: 1

WHAT YOU WILL NEED...

- Cotton pillowcase and sheet
- Fusible adhesive web
- Old newspapers and a spare sheet
- Iron
- Cotton fabrics: scraps of selection of prints
- Sewing thread to match fabrics
- Sewing workbasket (see page 15)

Embellishing bed linen is a brilliant way of using up tiny scraps of cotton fabric.

1 Gather together all your fabric scraps and launder any new pieces. Decide on two colors for your main theme—I went for pink and blue—and pick out a selection of patterned cottons in these shades.

2 Trace the 20 circle outlines on page 156 onto the paper side of the fusible adhesive web, using a sharp pencil. The pillowcase uses one hundred circles, so you will need to trace the page five times. Cut out each of the circles roughly, leaving a border of about ¼ inch around each one.

3 Protect your table with a thick layer of opened-out newspapers covered by a spare folded sheet: this will be your temporary ironing board. Iron the dots onto the wrong side of the various fabrics, choosing the most interesting areas of the printed designs, and cut out along the pencil lines.

4 Spread out your pillowcase on the sheet. Peel off the backing papers and arrange the circles randomly across the pillowcase with the adhesive side facing downward. Press them in place with a warm iron.

5 Edge each circle with straight stitches (see page 20 and detail on opposite page), using matching sewing thread.

6 The edge of the sheet is decorated in the same way. For a narrow border, as shown, cut about 70 circles for a double sheet and about 40 for a single sheet.

IF YOU DON'T WANT TO COVER THE PILLOWCASE COMPLETELY, USE FEWER CIRCLES AND ARRANGE THEM AS A BORDER OR IN A SIMPLE REPEATING PATTERN.

Songbird Bed Socks

Cath Kidston

SKILL RATING: 3

WHAT YOU WILL NEED...

- Pair of cashmere socks
- Lightweight nonwoven iron-on interfacing
- Dressmaker's disappearing-ink pen
- Iron and pressing cloth
- Embroidery floss in light brown, red, pink, dark brown, antique white, and green
- Sewing workbasket (see page 15)

These pretty bed socks are a real luxury and will keep your feet toasty warm all winter.

1 Enlarge the bird template on the right of page 162 by 120%. Place a 2-inch by 2½-inch rectangle of interfacing over the outline with the smooth (nonadhesive) facing upward. Use a disappearing-ink pen to draw over the lines, then snip the bird out around the outside edge.

2 Iron the cut-out bird to the side of one sock, just below the ribbing. Use a very cool iron and remember your pressing cloth to protect the soft fibers.

3 Thread a large-eyed needle with light brown embroidery floss. Embroider the bird's wings in three bands of satin stitch (see page 20), working between the ink lines. Next work the tail, body, and head, also in satin stitch. Look carefully at the photograph to check the colors and direction of the stitches.

4 Add the pink markings on the head in satin stitch, then work a few short stitches in dark brown for the eye, beak, and leg.

5 Finish off by filling in the rest of the head with white satin stitch and using the rest of the thread to work backstitch (see page 21) across the neck and between the body, tail, and wing. Work the branch in green backstitch.

6 Embroider a second bird on the other sock, reversing the image so that you have a matching pair.

SLIP ONE HAND INTO THE TOP OF THE SOCK TO SUPPORT THE FABRIC AS YOU EMBROIDER WITH THE OTHER — BUT TRY NOT TO PRICK YOUR FINGERS!

Detailed Pillowcases

Sweet dreams are guaranteed when you fall asleep on a flower-strewn pillow.

1 The two floral corner motifs are on page 168. I used them this size, but you can enlarge them slightly for a bolder look.

2 Trace the various elements onto fusible adhesive web, following the dotted lines on the larger flowers. Number each part of the design, then copy these numbers onto your tracing.

3 Cut out all the flowers, leaves, and dots roughly, and iron them onto the cotton fabrics. Refer to the colored diagram on page 167 for the right shades.

4 Trim each piece around the pencil line, but don't peel off the paper until you are ready to iron it in place: this way you can keep track of the numbering system.

5 The largest flower is the foundation for each flower grouping, so position this first, then position the two layers of petals and the dark center on top. Fix them in place with a warm iron, then add the smaller flowers and their centers. Finally, arrange the colored dots and the leaves around the flowers, and fuse in place.

6 Straight stitch around the edge of each large shape (see page 20), using matching sewing thread. Using embroidery floss, decorate the leaves with a single dark green straight stitch down the center, and the dots and flower centers with a simple cross-stitch (see page 20), using matching threads.

Cath Kidston

SKILL RATING: 2

WHAT YOU WILL NEED...

- Pair of laundered pillowcases
- Fusible adhesive web
- Iron
- Plain cotton fabric: scraps of pink, red, white, brown, green, yellow, orange, blue, and dark red
- Sewing thread to match fabrics
- Embroidery floss to match fabrics
- Sewing workbasket (see page 15)

THE CIRCUS FLOWER DESIGNS LOOK GOOD ON A LARGE OR SMALL SCALE; TAKE A LOOK AT THE DISHTOWEL ON PAGE 26 TO SEE THE SUPER-SIZED VERSION.

Flower-trimmed Pajamas

Cath Kidston

SKILL RATING: 2

WHAT YOU WILL NEED...

- Pair of cotton pajamas
- Lightweight nonwoven iron-on interfacing
- Dressmaker's disappearing-ink pen
- Iron and pressing cloth
- Embroidery floss in pink, red, and antique white
- Sewing workbasket (see page 15)

Red and pink embroidered flowers add a sweet, girly touch to a classic pair of cotton pajamas.

1 You'll find the templates for this project on page 166. Adjust the size so that they fit your pajamas: I reduced them both to 70% of the original.

2 Cut a strip of iron-on interfacing slightly larger than the row of flowers. Lay it over the photocopy with the smooth (nonadhesive) side facing upward. Trace the outlines with a disappearing-ink pen, then cut out the five flowers.

3 Fuse the flowers to the top of the pocket, with a cool iron—use a pressing cloth. Iron on the central large flower first, with the smooth side still facing upward, then position a small one on each side and another large one at each end of the row.

4 The embroidery is worked in satin stitch (see page 20). Sew the petals first in either red or pink, angling each block of stitches toward the center, then work the flower center in the other color.

5 Decorate the collar with the two sprigs, positioned so that the buds point inward. Embroider the flowers as before, in red with pink centers, and work the bud in pink satin stitch.

6 Stitch the leaves in antique white satin stitch, and work a single straight stitch down the center (see page 20). Embellish the bottoms by adding another sprig to the outer hems.

IF YOU LIKE THIS TYPE OF EMBROIDERY, TRY WORKING AN ELEGANT MONOGRAM ON ANOTHER PAIR OF PAJAMAS: YOU'LL FIND A FULL ALPHABET ON PAGE 159.

IF YOU ARE A KEEN STITCHER, YOU COULD ADD AN EMBROIDERED FLOWER BED TO THE GARDEN AND MAKE THE CLIMBING ROSES EVEN MORE ABUNDANT.

Country Cottage Pillow

Cath Kidston

SKILL RATING: 3

WHAT YOU WILL NEED...

- 18" square pillow cover
- Fusible adhesive web
- Iron and pressing cloth
- Tweed: 4" x 10" each of pink and red; scrap of brown
- Felt: 4" x 8" brown; 4" square each of green and stone; scraps of blue, yellow, white, and red
- Gingham: 4" square
- Sewing thread to match fabrics
- Dressmaker's disappearing-ink pen
- Embroidery floss in blue, antique white, brown, green, pink, and red
- Sewing workbasket (see page 15)

A new take on an old favorite: this pillow cover will add a touch of period country charm to your bedroom.

1 Enlarge the template on page 174 by 135%. Trace the cottage and the roof onto fusible adhesive web. Iron the cottage to pink tweed and the roof to red tweed. Cut out and peel off the backing. Fuse to the center of the cover, so the roof overlaps the cottage. Add the chimney in red and brown tweed.

2 For each window, cut the outer squares from brown felt, the inner squares from blue, and the curtains from gingham. Remove the papers, then iron on the brown squares, the blue squares, and the curtains. Anchor the brown felt and the curtains with a ring of straight stitches (see page 20), using matching sewing thread. Use blue embroidery floss to outline the inner edge of the curtains. Work two long straight stitches in white and brown for each window frame and anchor the centers with small diagonal stitches.

3 Cut out the felt details: green grass and hedges; brown porch, gate, and doorknob; stone path; yellow door; white fanlight and cloud. The wall is red tweed. Peel off the papers and position as follows: grass, path, porch, door, doorknob, fanlight, gate, wall, and hedges. Press and stitch in place.

4 Draw the lines for the roses, blue cloud, and birds with a disappearing-ink pen. Work the roses in chain, lazy daisy, and straight stitches, the cloud in chain stitch, and the birds in straight stitch, using appropriate colors (see pages 20–21). Complete the fanlight with brown straight stitches. Embroider the door knob. Make eight dots from red felt and two brown bricks, fuse to the hedge and wall, then add leaves in straight stitch.

DON'T FORGET YOUR PRESSING CLOTH WHEN YOU ARE FUSING ON THE APPLIQUÉ SHAPES: DIRECT HEAT FROM THE IRON COULD DAMAGE BOTH THE TWEED AND THE FELT.

Bags

I am a bag addict, not expensive designer bags, but great everyday shopping bags—there is nothing like a canvas tote. Take your pick of our designs to customize a dull-looking bag with stars, cowboys, or classic rose prints. You'll be spoiled for choice!

Flowery Tote

Cath Kidston

SKILL RATING: 1

WHAT YOU WILL NEED...

- Cotton tote bag
- Fusible adhesive web
- Iron
- Polka dot cotton fabric: small amount each of dark blue, light blue, pink, green, red, and yellow
- Small scissors/nail scissors
- Sewing thread to match fabrics
- Sewing workbasket (see page 15)

Transform a plain tote bag into an eco-friendly shopping bag by adding a scattering of polka dot flowers.

1 Enlarge the reversed flower templates on page 158 by 120%. Trace the outlines and center circles onto the paper side of the fusible adhesive web. I used 25 flowers, so traced the whole page twice, then added an extra bloom.

2 Cut out the flowers roughly, leaving a border of about ¼ inch around each one. With the adhesive side facing downward, iron them onto the back of the various fabrics.

3 Now cut the flowers out carefully around the outside edge. Snip out the center circles and peel off all the backing papers.

4 Lay the bag out on your ironing board and spread the flowers across the front. When you are happy with your arrangement, fuse them in place.

5 Decorate the inside and outside edges of each bloom with a round of straight stitches (see page 20), using matching sewing thread.

SHARP NAIL SCISSORS WITH CURVED BLADES ARE IDEAL FOR CUTTING OUT THE TINY FLOWER CENTERS.

Shiny Flowers
Cosmetic Bag

Cath Kidston

SKILL RATING: 1

WHAT YOU WILL NEED...

- White zip-up cosmetic bag
- Thin plastic-coated fabric: $3\frac{1}{4}$" square of light blue; 4" x 6" red
- Glue stick
- Sewing thread in red and blue
- Sewing workbasket (see page 15)

The design on this bag is floral without being fussy. You'll find that sewing with plastic-coated fabrics is no more difficult than working with cotton or felt.

1 Enlarge the flower templates at the foot of page 166 so that they fit your bag. Mine was 5 inches deep so I increased the size by 200%. Cut out one large and one small flower from your photocopy to use as a paper pattern.

2 Place the large flower on the reverse side of the red plastic-coated fabric and draw around it twice. Draw around the small flower once, on the back of the blue fabric.

3 Now cut the round flower center from the paper pattern. Draw around the large one twice on the blue fabric and the small one once on the red fabric. Cut all the shapes out around the pencil lines.

4 Fix the blue flower to the center of the bag using a small amount of adhesive from the glue stick. Add one red flower on each side, keeping the centers on the same level. Now glue the flower centers in place.

5 Secure the appliqué shapes by working a round of straight stitches around the edge of each one (see page 20), using either red or blue sewing thread.

USE A "SHARP" NEEDLE TO SEW DOWN THE FLOWERS AND ENSURE THAT YOU STITCH THROUGH THE BAG ONLY—NOT THE BULKY LINING.

IF YOU CAN'T FIND PLASTIC-COATED FABRIC, YOU COULD CUT THE STARS FROM WHITE COTTON FABRIC AND USE THE IRON-ON APPLIQUÉ TECHNIQUE TO SECURE THEM TO THE BAG.

Starry Tote

Cath Kidston

SKILL RATING: 1

WHAT YOU WILL NEED...

- Red tote bag
- Thin PVC fabric: 12" x 16" white
- Newspaper
- Polyvinyl acetate adhesive and paintbrush
- Sewing workbasket (see page 15)

Keep this sparkling tote folded up in your handbag and you'll never need a plastic shopping bag again!

1 Photocopy the outline template on page 154 and cut out five different-sized stars. Alternatively, you can trace them onto tracing paper.

2 Using a sharp pencil, draw around the paper stars on the back of the plastic-coated fabric 35 times, making sure you have a roughly equal number of each one. You may need to make more stars if your bag is larger than mine, which measures 14 inches by 16 inches.

3 Fold the newspaper so that it is the same size as your bag, then slip it inside. Place the bag on your work surface and arrange the stars across the front, shiny side up.

4 Stick each star down with a light coating of adhesive. Paint the glue over the back and wait until the surface feels tacky, rather than wet. Turn the star over and smooth it in place, pressing each point down with your fingertips.

CUT TWICE AS MANY STARS IF YOU WANT TO COVER BOTH SIDES OF YOUR BAG, BUT BE SURE TO LET THE GLUE DRY ON ONE SIDE BEFORE STARTING THE OTHER SIDE.

SEWING THROUGH CANVAS IS
TOUGH WORK, SO PUT THE
COWBOY MOTIF TOGETHER
BEFORE YOU ATTACH IT TO THE
BAG, TO SAVE YOUR FINGERS.

Cowboy Canvas Bag

The vintage cowboy rides again! This time on a roomy canvas bag, complete with a Western leather trim.

1 Enlarge the cowboy on page 150 to fit your bag, then trace him and his horse onto fusible adhesive web. Cut out roughly and fuse to light stone felt. Leave the backing paper on as you add the other pieces and remember to use your pressing cloth when ironing felt.

2 First dress the cowboy in a red tweed shirt, gingham kerchief, and blue jeans (remember the fusible adhesive web goes on the back of the fabric).

3 Use dark stone felt for the saddle, and the shadowed areas on the horse and Stetson. The boot, saddle strap and holster are cut from warm brown felt, with an extra detail on the holster in red tweed.

4 For the final layer, make the hooves, mane, bridle, and the cowboy's hair from peat brown felt. Now you can peel off the backing.

5 Anchor each piece to the main motif with straight stitches (see page 20), using sewing matching thread. Sew along only the inside edges of the shapes and around the details that fit within the outline (e.g., the boot and bridle) as the outside edge of the motif will be stitched to the bag.

6 Iron the finished motif in place on the front of the bag. Straight stitch all around the edge, using the appropriate color thread. Be careful not to stitch through the lining, if your bag has one.

7 Draw in the lasso with a disappearing-ink pen, and work over the line in chain stitch (see page 21), using red embroidery floss. Add tiny stitches in brown embroidery floss for the features on both horse and cowboy.

Cath Kidston

SKILL RATING: 3

WHAT YOU WILL NEED...

- Canvas bag
- Fusible adhesive web
- Iron and pressing cloth
- Felt: 8" square of light stone; 2" x 4" square each of dark stone, warm brown, and peat brown
- Woven fabric: scraps of red tweed, gingham, and denim
- Sewing thread to match fabrics
- Embroidery floss in red and brown
- Dressmaker's disappearing-ink pen
- Sewing workbasket (see page 15)

STITCH THROUGH THE CANVAS WITH A STABBING ACTION,
PUSHING THE NEEDLE IN AND OUT AT A RIGHT ANGLE.
IF YOU HAVEN'T USED A THIMBLE BEFORE, THIS MIGHT
BE A GOOD TIME TO START!

INTERPRET THESE VERSATILE ROSE MOTIFS IN YOUR OWN STYLE. COPY THE COLORED TEMPLATE, CUT THEM OUT, AND REARRANGE THEM IN A NEW DESIGN TO SUIT YOUR BAG.

Embroidered Evening Purse

Cath Kidston

SKILL RATING: 3

WHAT YOU WILL NEED...

- Fabric purse
- Dressmaker's disappearing-ink pen
- Lightweight nonwoven iron-on interfacing
- Iron and pressing cloth
- Embroidery floss in pink, red, antique white, green, and brown
- 2" square of fabric to match purse, for covering button
- ³⁄₄" self-cover button
- Sewing workbasket (see page 15)

Just the right size for your essentials, this purse makes a charming accessory for an evening out.

1 You will find the outline template for the rose swag on page 162. Check the size against your bag and adjust it on a photocopier if necessary.

2 Using a disappearing-ink pen, trace your chosen flowers and larger leaves onto iron-on interfacing. Cut them out carefully.

3 Position the motifs symmetrically around the flap, setting aside the center rose for the button and leaving a space for it. Iron them in place, using a pressing cloth. Fuse the rose to the center of the fabric square.

4 Mark in the stalks and smaller leaves with a disappearing-ink pen to complete the swag.

5 Start by working the pink parts of the roses in satin stitch (see page 20), then add the red petals. Work the flower centers in antique white straight stitches (see page 20).

6 Embroider the leaves in green floss and add a brown straight stitch to the center of each. Work the stems in green backstitch (see page 21).

7 Embroider the center rose on a small scrap of matching fabric in the same way, then cover the button according to the manufacturer's instructions. Sew it securely in place to complete the swag design.

YOU COULD LOOK OUT FOR A BEAUTIFUL VINTAGE BUTTON TO USE AS AN ALTERNATIVE TO THE EMBROIDERED ONE.

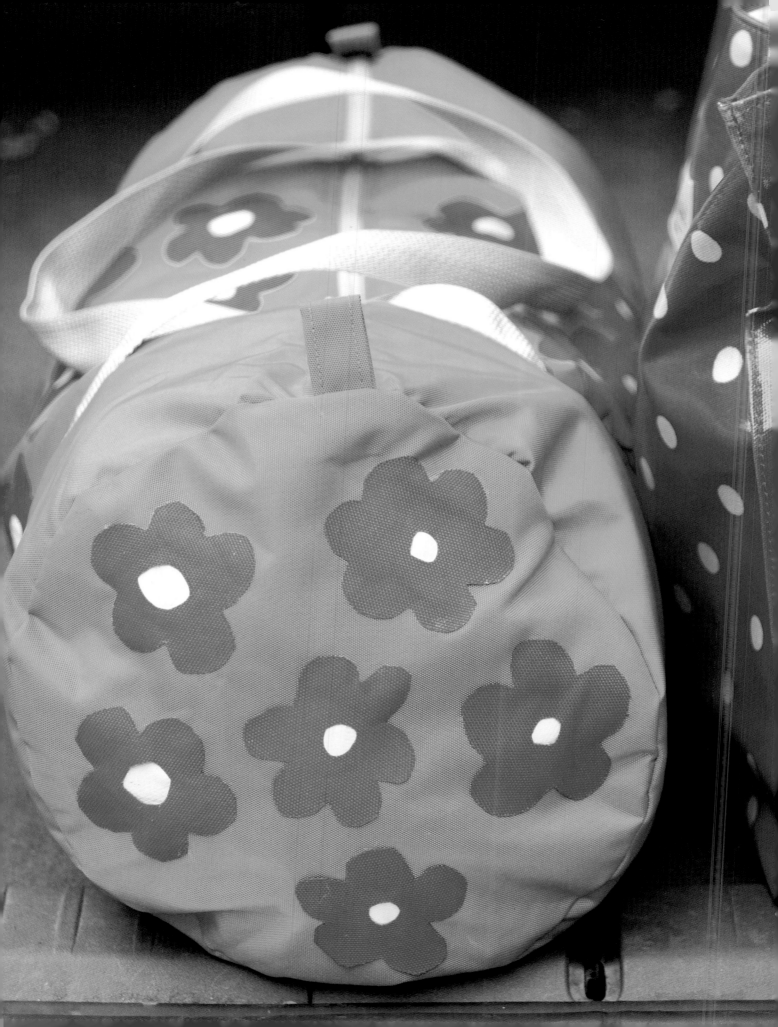

THE BRIGHT RED FLOWERS, WITH THEIR SHINY WHITE CENTERS, GIVE REAL VIBRANCY TO A PLAIN GREEN BAG, BUT A MULTICOLORED SELECTION WOULD LOOK EVEN MORE DAZZLING.

Floral Holdall

Cath Kidston

SKILL RATING: 1

WHAT YOU WILL NEED...

- Plain sport bag, 20" wide
- Small sheet of thin Bristol board
- Ballpoint pen
- Nylon fabric: 20" x 32" red
- Plastic-coated fabric: 15" x 25" white
- Polyvinyl acetate adhesive and paintbrush
- Sewing workbasket (see page 15)

If you pack your sports gear in this flowery holdall, a trip to the gym will become an uplifting event!

1 Choose five different flowers from the templates on page 158. Photocopy and trace them onto thin Bristol board, enlarging the size by 120%. Cut out around the edge and snip out the centers.

2 Draw around the inside and outside of the templates, directly onto the back of the red fabric. I used 45 flowers—nine of each size—on my bag, but you may need more for a larger holdall.

3 Now cut a circle of white plastic-coated fabric, about ³/₄ inch in diameter, to make a center for each flower.

4 Paint a thin layer of glue on the back of the first flower, just around the center hole. When it is almost dry, press a white circle, shiny side facing downward, onto the glue. Do the same with the other flowers.

5 When the glue has set, you can stick the flowers in place. Lay them, face down, on newspaper and coat the entire back with a thin layer of glue. Leave it until tacky, then press the flowers down firmly onto the bag, petal by petal. Start at the ends. Fix one flower to the center then surround it with a ring of five more. The other flowers are arranged around the main bag, in the space between the straps.

6 When you have finished, double-check all the flowers and glue down any areas that may have lifted.

TO GET THE WHITE CENTRAL PIECES THE RIGHT SIZE, DRAW AROUND A BOTTLE TOP OR LARGE COIN.

Strawberry Basket

Cath Kidston

SKILL RATING: 2

WHAT YOU WILL NEED...

- Cotton-lined basket
- Fusible adhesive web
- Iron and pressing cloth
- Felt: 8" square each of light red and dark red; 4" x 6" white; 4" square each of dark green and light green
- Sewing thread to match felts
- Glue stick
- Embroidery floss in light green and red
- Sewing workbasket (see page 15)

This useful basket, with its bold motif and patterned lining, embodies my love of vintage style given a contemporary twist.

1 The reversed strawberry templates are on page 170. I used the largest one for this project and increased its size just slightly to 110%, so that it looked in the right proportion to the basket.

2 Trace right around the motif (including the hull) onto fusible adhesive web and cut it out ¼ inch from the edge. Fuse the piece onto the light red felt. Always use a pressing cloth when working with felt. Cut out the strawberry accurately.

3 Now trace the outline for the dark red felt, following the dotted lines where the hull overlaps. Peel off the backing and iron to the main shape.

4 Cut the dark and light green hull pieces and iron them onto the strawberry. Finally, make the seeds from white felt and fuse them in place.

5 Peel the backing paper off the main shape and straight stitch (see page 20) around the seeds and along the inside edges of the dark red felt and the hull, using matching sewing thread. You don't need to stitch around the outside edge of the motif.

6 Position the finished motif centrally on one side of the basket, holding it in place with a few dabs from a glue stick. Straight stitch in place, using green or red embroidery floss. Sew through the basket with a stabbing action, being careful not to catch the lining.

A ROW OF THE THREE SMALLER STRAWBERRIES WOULD MAKE A GOOD ALTERNATIVE DECORATION FOR THIS RECTANGULAR BASKET.

Rose
Knitting Bag

Cath Kidston

SKILL RATING: 3

WHAT YOU WILL NEED...

- Knitting bag
- Fusible adhesive web
- Iron and pressing cloth
- Tweed: 8" square each of pink, red, and brown
- Sewing thread to match tweeds
- Dressmaker's disappearing-ink pen
- Embroidery floss in dark brown
- Sewing workbasket (see page 15)

Now that knitting is once again fashionable, you will need a suitable bag in which to keep your work.

1 The reversed outline motif for this project is on page 164. I used it at the given size for my bag, but you may wish to make it larger.

2 Start by tracing the two roses onto fusible adhesive web. Cut the shapes out roughly and iron them onto the pink and red tweed, using a pressing cloth. Cut out accurately, remove the backing, and position them on the bag, tucking the red rose under the edge of the pink one.

3 Now trace the leaves, ignoring the vein lines. You might find it helps to number each one as you draw it and mark these numbers on the outline, as they all look very similar.

4 Peel the paper off each leaf in turn and arrange them around the roses. Tuck some of them under the edges of the roses, where indicated by the dotted lines. Iron the flowers and leaves to the bag, using a pressing cloth.

5 Next add red tweed petals to the pink rose and pink tweed petals to the red rose. Once again you'll find it helpful to number them as you work. Sew around each shape in straight stitch (see page 20), using matching sewing thread.

6 The brown petal detail is embroidered. Referring to the colored template, draw the shapes in with a disappearing-ink pen, then work over them in satin stitch (see page 20), using brown embroidery floss.

TWEED IS A WOVEN FABRIC AND SO TENDS TO FRAY MORE THAN NONWOVEN FELT. HANDLE THE CUT-OUT SHAPES CAREFULLY, ESPECIALLY WHEN REMOVING THE BACKING PAPER.

Floral Drawstring Bag

Cath Kidston

SKILL RATING: 1

WHAT YOU WILL NEED...

- Drawstring bag
- Fusible adhesive web
- Cotton fabric print: 10" square
- Iron
- Sewing thread to match fabric
- Sewing workbasket (see page 15)

Simple bags like this have endless uses, especially when traveling. Why not make one to protect your favorite shoes?

1 Turn to page 158 to find the reversed outline motifs. To fit my bag, which is 11 inches by 12 inches, I increased the size to 120% and used 17 flowers: create your own look by making the blooms smaller or larger.

2 Iron fusible adhesive web onto the wrong side of the cotton fabric, then cut each flower out around the inner and outer lines.

3 Peel off the backing papers and lay the flowers across the front of the bag. Shuffle them around until you have a pleasing arrangement—you may need to add a couple extra or take one or two away. Fuse the flowers in place with a warm iron.

4 To secure the edges, work a round of short straight stitches around each flower (see page 20), using matching sewing thread.

APPLIQUÉ IS A WONDERFUL WAY TO RECYCLE FORGOTTEN FABRICS: HERE I USED A REMNANT OF VINTAGE FLORAL DRESS PRINT TO ADD COLOR AND PATTERN TO A PLAIN BAG.

Clothing

There is nothing more pleasing than recycling an old piece of clothing to give it a whole new lease on life. A good trick is to dye it first—perhaps start with an old white T-shirt than has gone a little gray. It's great fun seeing it transformed in the dye bucket. Then add a finishing touch of appliqué!

College Sweater

Cath Kidston

SKILL RATING: 1

WHAT YOU WILL NEED...

- Finely knit turquoise sweater
- Fusible adhesive web
- Iron and pressing cloth
- Felt: $2\frac{1}{2}$" x $4\frac{3}{4}$" pink
- Embroidery floss in red and pink
- Sheet of paper
- Cotton fabric print: 6" x 8"
- Sewing workbasket (see page 15)

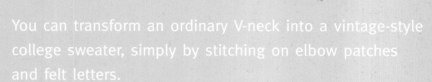

You can transform an ordinary V-neck into a vintage-style college sweater, simply by stitching on elbow patches and felt letters.

1 Choose your initials from the reversed template on page 160, enlarge as necessary, and trace onto fusible adhesive web. Cut the letters out roughly.

2 Place the letters, adhesive-side down, on the felt. Lay a pressing cloth over the top, then fuse them in place with a warm iron. Cut out accurately.

3 Peel away the backing paper from each letter. Place the sweater on your ironing board and position the letters, right side up, to the right of the neckline. Iron them in place, again using a pressing cloth.

4 Using red embroidery floss, work a round of straight stitches (see page 20) around the edge of each letter to secure the felt and to add extra decoration.

5 To make the template for the patches, cut a 3-inch-by-6-inch rectangle of paper. Fold it in quarters, then draw a curve across the unfolded corners. Cut along this line, through all the layers, then open out the paper.

6 Draw around the outline of the template twice, on the paper side of the fusible adhesive web. Iron the adhesive side to the wrong side of the printed fabric, then cut out the patches along the pencil lines.

7 Remembering your pressing cloth, iron the patches to the back of the sleeves, making sure they are both at the same level. Embellish the edges with blanket stitch (see page 21), using pink embroidery floss.

ABCDE

TO POSITION THE PATCHES, TURN THE EDGE OF THE CUFF
UP TO THE SHOULDER LINE, THEN PLACE THE CENTER OF THE
PATCH ALONG THE FOLD.

IF YOU LIKE, YOU CAN APPLIQUÉ ALL THE WAY AROUND THE HEM (YOU'LL NEED TO ALLOW MORE FELT FOR THIS) OR JUST SEW A FEW MOTIFS TO THE FRONT OF YOUR SKIRT.

Cowboy Skirt

Cath Kidston

SKILL RATING: 3

WHAT YOU WILL NEED...

- Red skirt
- Fusible adhesive web and iron
- Iron and pressing cloth
- Felt: 10" square each of light stone, warm brown, light green, and dark green; 4" square each of peat brown, dark stone, and red
- Woven fabric: scraps of blue gingham, denim, and red tweed
- Sewing thread to match fabrics
- Embroidery floss in dark brown, mid blue, light blue, and green
- Dressmaker's disappearing-ink pen
- Sewing workbasket (see page 15)

Even if you're not off to a rodeo, hoedown or line dancing session, this swingy skirt will put a spring in your step!

1 Enlarge the reversed templates on page 150 by 115%. Trace around the cowboy and horse onto fusible adhesive web, cut out roughly, and fuse onto light stone felt. Cut out accurately, peel off the paper and iron onto the skirt, 6 inches from the hem and a little off to the side. Make sure you always use a pressing cloth when you're working with felt.

2 Now build up the details, starting with gingham shirt and denim jeans. The cowboy's hair, the horse's mane, bridle, and hooves are peat brown felt, and the shadows on its body, the saddle, and the hat dark stone.

3 Use warm brown felt for the main holster, saddle strap, and the boot, and red tweed for the holster detail and the neckerchief. Straight stitch (see page 20) around each piece in matching sewing thread, then work the facial details in dark brown embroidery floss.

4 Draw the dust cloud, lasso, and grass tufts with a disappearing-ink pen and chain stitch (see page 21) over the lines: mid blue for the lasso, light blue for the cloud, and dark green for the grass.

5 For the cactuses, trace the outline onto fusible adhesive web, and cut it out from light green felt. Add the shadows in dark green, following the inner lines. Stitch around each piece in green thread. Use warm brown felt to make the main wagon shape, then add the canopy in red and the remaining highlights in white. Edge each individual piece in matching thread. Chain stitch the grass with dark green embroidery thread.

6 Decorate the back of the skirt with a two more cactuses, and a wagon cut from warm brown felt with details in red and light stone.

CHOOSE A FULL, GATHERED SKIRT IN A HEAVY COTTON WEAVE FOR THAT AUTHENTIC COWGIRL LOOK.

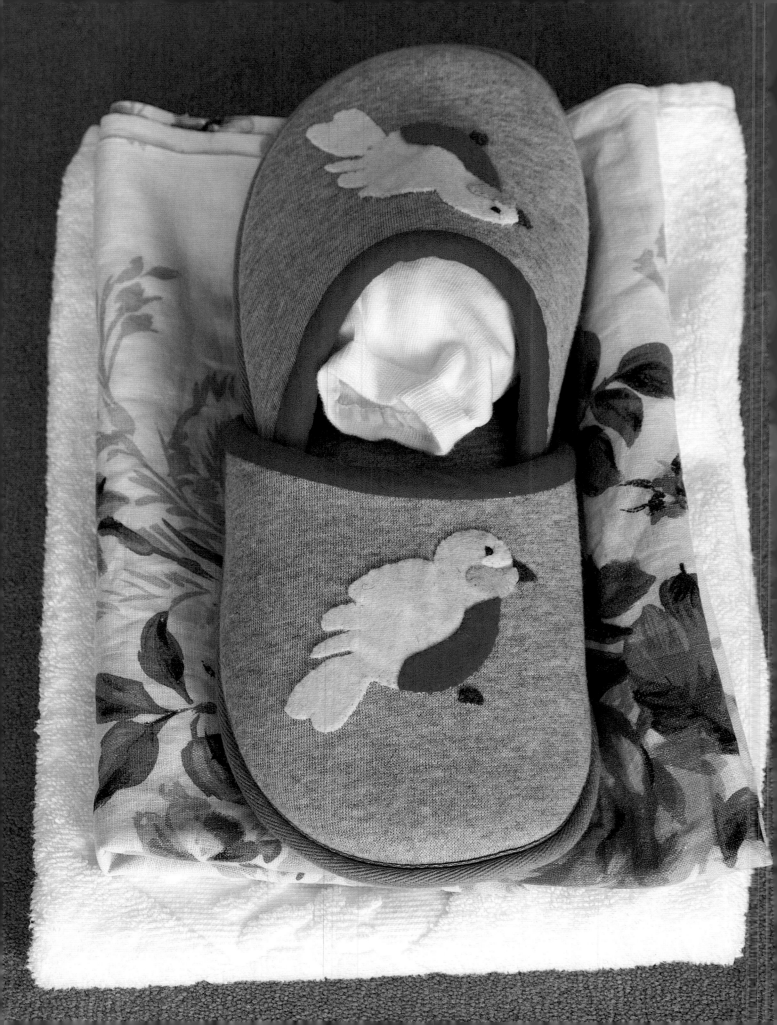

THE FLYING SONGBIRDS THAT APPEAR WITH THIS MOTIF ON PAGE 162 WOULD BE A GOOD ALTERNATIVE DESIGN. YOU COULD EVEN SWAP THE COLORS AROUND TO MAKE THEM INTO BLUEBIRDS.

Songbird Slippers

Cath Kidston

SKILL RATING: 2

WHAT YOU WILL NEED...

- Pair of plain slippers
- Fusible adhesive web
- Iron and pressing cloth
- Felt: 4" x 6" light stone; scraps of red, dark brown, pink, and white
- Sewing thread to match felts
- Embroidery floss in dark brown
- Sewing workbasket (see page 15)

Pad about the house to your heart's content in these customized slippers.

1 You'll find the songbird motif on page 162. I enlarged it by 200%, to 2³/₄ inches tall to fit these gray jersey slippers, but you may wish to make it slightly larger or smaller.

2 Trace around the complete bird outline onto fusible adhesive web. Cut out roughly, fuse (using a pressing cloth) onto light stone felt, and snip around the pencil line.

3 Now cut out the red breast, brown beak, and the pink and white head details. Peel the papers off these four pieces and carefully iron them in place on the main bird shape, again using a pressing cloth. Remove the backing from the bird and pin it to the center front of the left slipper.

4 Work a round of straight stitches around each piece (see page 20), using matching sewing thread. Add a tiny brown felt shape for the foot and work a few stitches in dark brown embroidery floss for the eye.

5 Decorate the right slipper in the same way, reversing the template so that the two birds are facing each other.

IF PINNING THE FELT TO THE SLIPPER FABRIC PROVES A LITTLE TRICKY, TRY USING A DAB OF ADHESIVE FROM A GLUE STICK TO KEEP IT IN PLACE AS YOU SEW.

IF YOU CAN'T FIND A SCARF OR THROW IN THE RIGHT COLOR FOR THIS PROJECT, BUY A 16-INCH LENGTH OF JERSEY OR WOOL FABRIC INSTEAD.

Racing Car Scarf

Cath Kidston

SKILL RATING: 2

WHAT YOU WILL NEED...

- Strawberry pink scarf
- Fusible adhesive web
- Iron and pressing cloth
- Lightweight tweed: 8" square of brown; 4" square of red
- Felt: scraps of beige, pale beige, and dark brown
- Dressmaker's disappearing-ink pen
- Sewing thread to match fabrics
- Embroidery floss in brown
- 4 brown buttons, for the wheels
- Sewing workbasket (see page 15)

Wait for the checkered flag to go down...

1 Trace the all elements that make up the top racing car outline on page 146 onto fusible adhesive web. Draw the driver's head and shoulders in a single piece following the dotted line, then his helmet and jacket separately. Cut out the pieces, about ¼ inch from the outlines.

2 Iron the adhesive side of the two car parts onto the brown tweed and cut around the edge. Remember to snip the small slit across the hood of the car.

3 Now cut the helmet, jacket, and wheels from red tweed, and make the side vent, hubcaps, and oval from beige felt. The driver is in pale beige felt and his goggles, the steering wheel, and seat back are brown felt. Remember to use a pressing cloth whenever you are ironing felt.

4 Remove the backing papers. Center the two parts of the car at one end of the scarf, 5 inches from the hem. Iron in place, then add the wheels and hubcaps. Fuse the driver in position and add his goggles, helmet, and jacket. Finish with his seatback, vent, and the oval.

5 Edge each shape with a round of straight stitches (see page 20), using matching sewing thread.

6 Draw a number onto the oval with a disappearing-ink pen and straight stitch over it, using brown embroidery floss. Finish off by sewing a button to the center of each hubcap.

7 Decorate the other end of the scarf in the same way with the second racing car. Reverse the outline so that it is going in the opposite direction.

IF YOU FIND THE BROWN FELT DETAILS A LITTLE DIFFICULT TO CUT ACCURATELY, YOU COULD EMBROIDER THEM IN SATIN STITCH INSTEAD (SEE PAGE 20).

IF YOU PREFER A MORE FLOWERY LOOK, CHOOSE A PRINTED FABRIC TO MAKE YOUR STARS.

Starry T-shirt

Cath Kidston

SKILL RATING: 1

WHAT YOU WILL NEED...

- Laundered cotton T-shirt
- Fusible adhesive web
- Iron
- Woven cotton fabric: scraps of plain colors, washed and pressed
- Thread braid or assorted spools of sewing thread
- Sewing workbasket (see page 15)

Give yourself maximum star rating with a shooting star T-shirt.

1 Turn to the star outlines on page 154, and trace 60 stars in different sizes onto the paper side of your fusible adhesive web. Cut each one out roughly.

2 Gather together your fabric pieces and iron the adhesive side of the stars onto a selection of your favorite colors. Cut them all out, following the pencil line precisely.

3 Lay the top of the T-shirt across your ironing board and arrange the stars over the sleeves and around the neckline, reserving about 16 for the back of the sleeves. Move them around until you have a good balance of size and color across the design.

4 Iron the stars in place, one at a time, starting at the bottom edge of the arrangement. Peel the backing paper off each one in turn and press them with the tip of the iron. Decorate the back of the sleeves in the same way.

5 Add even more color to the twinkling stars by securing them with contrasting sewing thread. Sew a round of short straight stitches around each star, working the stitches at right angles to the stars (see page 20).

THE MORE FABRICS YOU HAVE, THE MORE EFFECTIVE THIS DESIGN WILL BE, BUT KEEP THEM ALL WITHIN THE SAME TONAL RANGE.

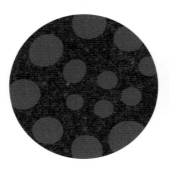
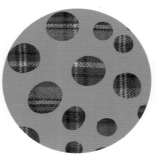

Polka Dot Beret

Cath Kidston

SKILL RATING: 1

WHAT YOU WILL NEED...

- Red beret
- Fusible adhesive web
- Iron and pressing cloth
- Felt: 6" x 12" white
- Embroidery floss in white
- Sewing workbasket (see page 15)

Bring out your inner pixie with this fun polka dot toadstool beret.

1 Trace the largest outline circle on page 156 onto the paper side of the fusible adhesive web 14 times. Cut each circle out roughly, about $\frac{1}{4}$ inch from the edge.

2 Fuse the adhesive side of the circles onto the white felt, placing the cloth over the fabric first, so that the heat of the iron won't distort the felt. Carefully cut out each one, following the pencil line closely.

3 Peel the backing papers off the circles. Spacing them evenly, arrange five of them around the beret's stalk. Press them in place with a warm iron, again using a protective cloth.

4 Arrange the remaining circles in a second ring, just outside the first. Iron them in place as before.

5 Secure each circle in place with a round of straight stitches (see page 20), using white embroidery floss. Sew with a large-eyed needle that will pass easily through the thick wool fabric.

YOU DON'T HAVE TO USE THE CIRCLES, OF COURSE. MAYBE YOU'D PREFER STARS, FLOWERS, OR EVEN TINY DOG-BONE SHAPES!

Boat T-shirt

Cath Kidston

SKILL RATING: 3

WHAT YOU WILL NEED...

- Laundered cotton T-shirt
- Fusible adhesive web
- Iron and pressing cloth
- Felt: 4" x 10" white; 2$\frac{1}{2}$" x 10" blue; 4" square of red; 1$\frac{1}{4}$" x 4" yellow; scraps of green and brown
- Sewing thread to match felts
- Dressmaker's disappearing-ink pen
- Embroidery floss in mid blue, dark brown, and red
- Sewing workbasket (see page 15)

Prepare for a life on the open waves with this jaunty, nautical T-shirt, just perfect for a seaside holiday.

1 Start by tracing the cloud on page 152 onto the paper side of the fusible adhesive web. Cut out roughly and iron the adhesive to white felt. Always use a pressing cloth to protect the felt. Cut along the outline, remove the paper, and iron the felt onto the T-shirt. Using white thread, sew short straight stitches all around the edge of the cloud (see page 20).

2 Trace all the waves onto fusible adhesive web, cut out roughly around the outside edge, then fuse onto the blue felt. Cut out the long top wave, peel off the backing, and iron it on just below the horizon. Add the other waves, one at a time, and secure with blue thread.

3 Next, cut out the red and the yellow felt sails. Iron them in position and add the white stripes. Stitch in place with straight stitches, using matching sewing thread.

4 Cut out and iron on the three tiny pennants for the small boats, then finish off with the four hulls in the appropriate colored felt. Secure with straight stitches, using matching sewing thread.

5 The details are worked with embroidery floss. Work blue chain stitch (see page 21) around the top edge of the clouds, working on the T-shirt, along the blue outline shown in the colored template.

6 Using a disappearing-ink pen, draw in the other details—the masts, the seagulls, and the pennant on the large boat. Using embroidery floss, work straight stitches over these lines: brown for the masts and seagulls, and red for the pennant.

Kids

An item like this beautiful appliquéd blanket will become a treasured heirloom. If you don't have the patience to make such a large piece, try the technique on a small bag or sweatshirt. With an older sister, I had endless hand-me-downs, and I wish my mother had given my clothes such exciting updates!

Floral Dress

Cath Kidston

SKILL RATING: 3

WHAT YOU WILL NEED...

- Simple tunic dress
- Lightweight nonwoven iron-on interfacing
- Dressmaker's disappearing-ink pen
- Iron and pressing cloth
- Embroidery floss in purple, light orange, brown, stone, pink, red, green, and turquoise
- Sewing workbasket (see page 15)

This adorable tunic dress has a timeless charm, which will guarantee that any little girl who wears it gets off to a head start in the fashion stakes.

1 The floral embroidery is deceptively simple to work. Read the detailed instructions on pages 22–23 to find out how it is done, then turn to page 168 of the template section.

2 Using a disappearing-ink pen, trace two large and six small flower outlines onto the smooth side of the iron-on interfacing, ignoring the dotted lines. You will also need eight large and four small leaves. Cut all the motifs out around the outside edge.

3 Arrange the shapes in the corners of the yoke of the dress, either following the photograph on the left or adapting the design to suit your particular dress. Iron them in place, using a pressing cloth.

4 Embroider all the flowers in satin stitch (see page 20). Fill in each area of each shape with a block of stitches following the colors used on the opposite page, and angling the stitches toward the center of the flowers.

TINY DETAILS ADD CHARACTER: NOTE HOW THE BUTTONHOLES
ARE OUTLINED WITH GREEN THREAD AND QUIRKY
REPLACEMENT BUTTONS COMPLEMENT THE EMBROIDERY.

Cowboy Denim Jacket

Cath Kidston

SKILL RATING: 3

WHAT YOU WILL NEED...

- Denim jacket
- Fusible adhesive web
- Iron and pressing cloth
- Felt: 8" square of light stone; 4" square each of red, blue, dark stone, brown, light green, and dark green
- Embroidery floss to match felts
- Chalk pencil
- Sewing workbasket (see page 15)

Be part of your own Wild West adventure with a customized cowboy jacket. Yee-ha!

1 Trace the cowboy and his horse on page 150 onto fusible adhesive web. Cut out roughly, iron onto light stone felt, then cut along the pencil line. Take off the backing and iron the motif to the center of the back of the jacket. Always use a pressing cloth when working with felt.

2 Make the cowboy's shirt from red felt and his leg from blue as above, then fuse them onto the main motif.

3 The next layer is of dark stone felt: use this for the shadows on the horse, the saddle, scarf, and hat. The boot, hooves, mane, bridle, pistol, and strap details are in brown felt. Finally, make the holster from red felt.

4 Secure each piece of the finished appliqué with a round of short straight stitches, worked at right angles to the edge (see page 20). Use all six strands of the stranded embroidery floss and match the colors to the felt.

5 With brown floss, embroider straight-stitch details onto the cowboy's hat and hair. Work two tiny stitches for his eyes, and pairs of stitches for the horse's eye and nostril. Outline the saddle in backstitch.

6 With a chalk pencil, draw in the dust cloud, grass, and lasso. Embroider over the lines, using blue backstitch for the cloud, green straight stitch for the grass, and light stone-colored chain stitch for the lasso (see page 21).

7 For the cactus on the pocket, make the main shape from light green felt and the shadow from dark green. Edge both layers with matching straight stitches as before, then embroider the flowers in red and the grass in green.

THIS JACKET FITS A CHILD AGED TWO TO THREE: IF YOU ARE MAKING IT FOR AN OLDER CHILD YOU SHOULD ENLARGE THE TEMPLATE SO THAT IT FILLS THE WHOLE OF BACK PANEL.

IF YOU ARE MAKING THIS TOP AS A BIRTHDAY GIFT, YOU COULD CHANGE THE NUMBER EMBROIDERED ON THE FELT OVAL TO THE CHILD'S AGE.

Racing Car Sweatshirt

Make this for the boy racer in your life—even if his favorite vehicle is still only a tricycle!

1 Turn to the reversed outlines on page 146. Trace all the parts that make up the driver and his car, the two trees, the hedge, grass, and fence onto fusible adhesive web, then add an extra tree. Cut the pieces out roughly.

2 Iron the fusible adhesive web to the various felts: the car, jacket, helmet, and fence onto red; the wheels, seat, steering wheel, goggles, and trunks to brown; the oval, vent, and hubcaps to stone; the trees, hedge, and tuft of grass to green. Cut out the motifs accurately, and remove the paper backings as you need the pieces.

3 Spread the sweatshirt out on your ironing board. Position the car across the chest. Tuck a tree trunk under the boot and fuse in place.

4 Add the wheels and driver, then fuse on his helmet, goggles, and jacket, the steering wheel and seatback, the vent, the oval, and finally, the hubcaps.

5 Finish off by arranging the countryside motifs on either side as shown: two trees and the grass to the right; the hedge, fence, and third tree to the left. Tuck the trunks under the trees and place the fence over the hedge.

6 Anchor each felt shape with short straight stitches (see page 20), using matching sewing thread. Lastly, draw on the details with disappearing-ink pen and work with embroidery floss: light stone and brown backstitch (see page 21) on the wheels and for the number, blue straight stitch on the vent, and light stone satin stitch (see page 20) for the windshield.

Cath Kidston

SKILL RATING: 2

WHAT YOU WILL NEED...

- Gray cotton sweatshirt
- Fusible adhesive web
- Iron and pressing cloth
- Felt: 8" x 4" green; 6" square of red; 4" square each of brown and dark stone
- Sewing thread to match felts
- Embroidery floss in light stone, brown, and blue
- Dressmaker's disappearing-ink pen
- Sewing workbasket (see page 15)

THE TREES AND OTHER COUNTRYSIDE MOTIFS HAVE BEEN REARRANGED TO SUIT THIS DESIGN. LAY THEM OUT FIRST TO CHECK THE SPACING AND HOW THE FINAL DESIGN WILL LOOK.

Antique Cardigan

Cath Kidston

SKILL RATING: 3

WHAT YOU WILL NEED...

- Finely knit cream V-neck cardigan
- Lightweight nonwoven iron-on interfacing
- Dressmaker's disappearing-ink pen
- Iron and pressing cloth
- Embroidery floss in pink, red, antique white, and green
- Sewing workbasket (see page 15)

Turn a plain garment into a keepsake to hand down through the generations.

1 Photocopy the flower motifs on page 162, increasing the size to 115%. Make a second enlarged copy that is a mirror image of the first. Trace one large and three small roses, plus three buds, from each sheet onto the smooth (nonadhesive) side of the iron-on interfacing, using a disappearing-ink pen.

2 Cut out all the flowers and arrange them symmetrically on either side of the neckline. Fuse in place with an iron, using a pressing cloth to protect the cardigan.

3 You'll find detailed instructions on how to embroider over lightweight nonwoven iron-on interfacing on page 23. Read through these, then fill in the rose and bud outlines with pink, red, and antique white satin stitch (see page 20). Add a few green stitches to the center of each rose.

4 Embroider the leaves in satin stitch, angling the stitches toward the center vein, and finish off by working the stems in backstitch (see page 21).

THIS IS A PROJECT FOR AN EXPERIENCED STITCHER, BUT IF YOU ARE A BEGINNER, INCREASE THE SIZE OF THE ROSES BY 200% AND EMBROIDER THEM ON A LARGE SCALE.

IF YOU DON'T HAVE THE TIME TO STITCH THE ENTIRE ALPHABET, WORK JUST A TWO-LETTER MONOGRAM IN THE CENTER OF THE COVER.

Alphabet Pillow

Nearly as easy to make as ABC, this pillow would be a wonderful nursery accessory.

1 Enlarge the reversed letters on page 160 by 250% so that they are 3 inches tall. Trace all of them except D, H, S, U, and V onto the paper side of the fusible adhesive web and cut out about ¼ inch from the edge.

2 Iron the letters onto the various felt pieces, then cut out neatly. Always use a pressing cloth when working with felt. Cut the remaining letters from the photocopy and turn them the right side up.

3 Spread the newspapers on your work surface with the dishtowel on top to make an impromptu ironing board. Lay the pillow cover over the dishtowel.

4 Peel the paper from the felt letters and position both these and the paper cutouts across the cover, referring to the picture opposite as a placement guide. Pin the paper letters in place and iron the felt letters in place, using a pressing cloth.

5 Draw around each paper letter with a disappearing-ink pen and then unpin them. Embroider over these outlines in chain stitch (see page 21). Work a round of contrasting blanket stitch around each felt letter (see page 21).

Cath Kidston

SKILL RATING: 3

WHAT YOU WILL NEED...

- 18" cream pillow cover
- Fusible adhesive web
- Iron and pressing cloth
- Felt: 4" x 12" each of pale pink, dark pink, mid blue, light blue, green, yellow, and brown
- Old newspapers and dishtowel
- Dressmaker's disappearing-ink pen
- Embroidery floss to match felts
- Sewing workbasket (see page 15)

USE THE FINISHED PHOTOGRAPH AS YOUR GUIDE TO CHOOSING COLORS FOR THE FELT LETTERS AND THEIR EMBROIDERED EDGINGS, OR CHOOSE YOUR OWN COLOR SCHEME.

Starry Bib

Cath Kidston

SKILL RATING: 1

WHAT YOU WILL NEED...

- White terry cloth bib
- Fusible adhesive web
- Iron
- Plain cotton fabric: 4" square each of green, pink, yellow, and blue
- Sewing thread to match fabrics
- Sewing workbasket (see page 15)

This shooting star bib will bring a touch of sophistication to the messiest lunchtime!

1 The outline star templates are on page 154. Use a sharp pencil to trace them onto the paper side of the fusible adhesive web, then add three more so that you have 22 in all. Cut all of the stars out roughly.

2 Using the correct iron temperature for your fabrics, iron five or six stars onto each of the cotton fabrics. Trim them neatly around the pencil lines.

3 Lay the bib out flat on your ironing board. Peel the backing papers from the stars and arrange them on the bib using the photograph opposite as a guide. Fuse them in place with a cool iron.

4 Anchor the stars with straight stitches around the edge of each one (see page 20), using matching sewing thread.

BABIES HAVE NO RESPECT FOR THEIR BEST OUTFITS,
SO THE BIB WILL INEVITABLY NEED FREQUENT WASHING.
SOAK IT IN GENTLE STAIN REMOVER AS NECESSARY, AND
LAUNDER ON A COOL CYCLE.

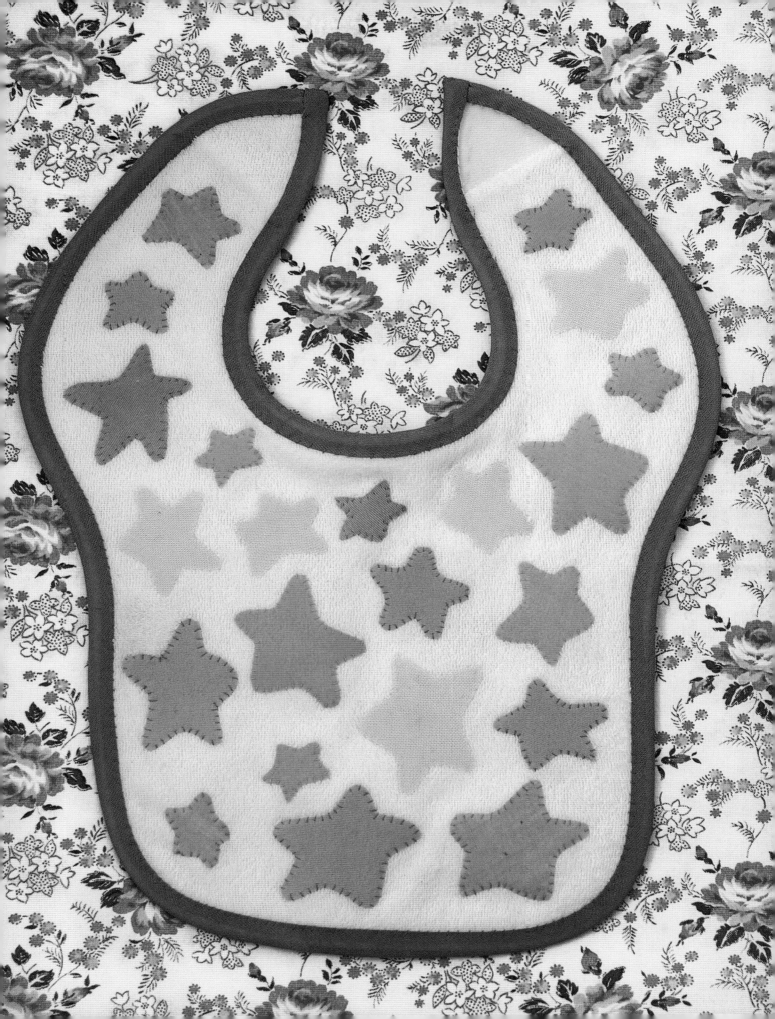

Tiny Tote

Cath Kidston

SKILL RATING: 2

WHAT YOU WILL NEED...

- Small tweed tote bag
- Fusible adhesive web
- Iron and pressing cloth
- Cotton fabric: 6" x 8" red polka dot; 4" x 6" green polka dot; 4" x 10" floral
- Felt: scrap of brown
- Sewing thread to match fabrics
- Sewing workbasket (see page 15)

Little girls love to keep their treasures in a special bag, so these little totes are guaranteed to delight.

1 Enlarge the flower basket template on page 166 to fit your bag's proportions: I increased the size by 230% for my $9\frac{1}{2}$-inch-square tote.

2 Using a sharp pencil, trace the basket, handle, leaves, flowers, and their centers onto the paper side of the fusible adhesive web. Cut the shapes out roughly.

3 Iron the fusible-adhesive-web pieces onto the wrong side of the fabrics: the basket and handle go on the red polka dot cotton; the leaves on the green polka dot fabric, and the flowers on the floral print. Fuse the flower centers to the felt, using a pressing cloth.

4 Cut out all the shapes and carefully remove the backing papers. Position the basket near the bottom of your bag, then place the handle a short distance above it.

5 Arrange the three flowers so that they overlap the areas indicated by the dotted lines. Put the leaves in place, tucking them under the flowers where shown, and finally, add the flower centers. Iron the completed design onto the bag, remembering your pressing cloth to protect the background.

6 Referring to the diagram on page 165, sew each appliqué shape to the bag with a round of straight stitches (see page 20), using matching sewing thread.

THIS FOLK-ART-STYLE MOTIF WOULD WORK EQUALLY WELL ON THE FRONT OF A T-SHIRT OR PERHAPS ON A COTTON APRON FOR BUDDING CHEFS.

Racing Car Blanket

Cath Kidston

SKILL RATING: 2

WHAT YOU WILL NEED...

- Blue single-bed blanket
- Fusible adhesive web
- Iron and pressing cloth
- Felt: for each motif (see below):
6" square of red or blue for car;
4 x 8" light green; 4" square of each
of brown and dark stone; 2 x 3" red
for fence
- Sewing thread to match felt
- Embroidery floss in stone, brown,
  and blue
- Sewing workbasket (see page 15)

The procession of vintage cars along the border of this cozy blanket will inspire endless bedtime tales of record-breaking racers.

1 The racing car motifs are on page 146: the outline versions are both traveling in the same direction. With a pencil, trace all the elements of the top car onto fusible adhesive web and cut them out roughly.

2 Start with the red car. Iron the fusible adhesive web onto felt: red for the car, helmet, and jacket; brown for the wheels, steering wheel, and goggles; stone for the driver, windshield, oval, vent, and hubcaps. Use a pressing cloth when working with felt. Trim carefully around each pencil line.

3 Peel away the backings and iron the two parts of the car centrally onto the blanket, $^3/_4$ inch from the satin binding. Add the driver, then his jacket, goggles, and helmet. Fuse on the other elements.

4 Secure every shape with straight stitches (see page 20), using matching sewing thread. The details are embroidered on with embroidery floss: stone and brown backstitch (see page 21) for the wheels and number, with blue straight stitch on the vent.

5 Now appliqué a blue car on each side of the first, leaving 3–4 inches between them. The detail on the hood is different for these cars and they do not have a vent—otherwise the method is just the same. Finally, add two more red cars toward the corners, with a similar gap between them.

6 Fill in the spaces between the cars with a trees, bushes, fences, and tufts of grass. Refer to the photograph opposite to see how to arrange these.

FIVE CARS FIT NEATLY ACROSS A SINGLE BLANKET **59** INCHES WIDE. MEASURE YOURS FIRST TO WORK OUT HOW MANY MOTIFS YOU'LL NEED AND HOW MUCH SPACE TO LEAVE BETWEEN THEM.

Gifts

There is nothing more touching than a home-made gift that has had care and thought put into it. Here are some ideas for things to make, and many are very quick—it's usually just a case of thinking ahead!

IF YOU LIKE THE LOOK OF THIS PICTURE, WHY NOT USE ONE OF THE OTHER DESIGNS IN THE SAME WAY — THE COTTAGE, PERHAPS, OR THE SONGBIRDS?

Framed Sailboats

SKILL RATING: 3

WHAT YOU WILL NEED...

- Old picture frame
- Linen: piece 1¼" larger all around than the frame's opening
- Fusible adhesive web
- Iron and pressing cloth
- Felt: 4" x 10" white; 8" x 10" blue; 8" square of red; 2" x 6" yellow; scraps of green and brown
- Embroidery floss to match felts
- Dressmaker's disappearing-ink pen
- Sewing workbasket (see page 15)

A nautical theme works anywhere in the house: these sailboats would look equally at home in a kitchen, bedroom, or living room.

1 Enlarge the reversed sailboat outline on page 152 to fit within your frame. Make a couple of copies at different sizes and choose the one that you like best.

2 Start by tracing the waves onto fusible adhesive web. Iron them onto blue felt and cut out. Always use a pressing cloth when working with felt. Peel the paper from the top wave and position it so that the horizon lies two thirds of the way down the frame. Now add the other waves.

3 Next, cut the sails from red and yellow felt. Iron them in position and add the white stripes and red pennants. Finish off by making the hulls from the appropriate color felt.

4 Stitch around each shape with straight stitches (see page 20), using matching embroidery floss. For the smaller sails, stitch right across each narrow white stripe, rather than sewing along each side.

5 Embroider the remaining details. Draw the cloud line (you'll see how far this extends on the colored template) with a disappearing-ink pen and stitch over it in blue chain stitch (see page 21). Work the seagulls, masts, and ropes in brown straight stitches.

THE SCRUFFIEST PICTURE FRAME CAN BE ENLIVENED WITH FRESH PAINT. SAND IT DOWN LIGHTLY, THEN BUY A SMALL SAMPLE POT OF PAINT AND APPLY TWO OR THREE COATS TO CONCEAL THE OLD FINISH.

IF YOUR DOG IS A FLUFFY FEMALE, YOU MAY PREFER TO CHANGE THE BOWL TO A PINK POLKA DOT BOWL VARIATION TO SUIT HER CHARACTER.

Dog Cushion

Cath Kidston

SKILL RATING: 1

WHAT YOU WILL NEED...

- Dog bed cushion
- Fusible adhesive web
- Iron and pressing cloth
- Felt: 6" x 10" each of brown and turquoise; 4" x 6" white; 8" square of red
- Linen: 4" x 10" off-white
- Sewing thread to match fabrics
- Sewing workbasket (see page 15)

Don't forget the family pet when it comes to giving presents. Every dog's favorite items—a ball, a bowl, and a bone—feature on this comfortable cushion.

1 Enlarge the three accessory outlines on page 148 by 300% so that they are on the right scale for the bed.

2 Trace the bowl, the oval detail, and the 13 dots onto the paper side of your fusible adhesive web. Cut out roughly and iron onto felt: turquoise for the bowl, brown for the oval detail, and white for the dots. Remember your pressing cloth. Cut out the motifs accurately.

3 Peel the backings from the oval and the dots, then fuse them to the bowl, following the colored template on page 147 for the positions.

4 Remove the paper from the bowl and secure the dots and oval with short straight stitches (see page 20), using matching sewing thread. Pin the bowl across one corner of the cushion and straight stitch in place.

5 Cut the bone from linen and its shadow details from brown felt. Take the paper off the shadows and iron them to the bone. Now remove the paper from the bone, pin it to the cushion to the right of the bowl, and secure with cream sewing thread.

6 Make the ball in red felt with brown curve details. Peel the backings off the curves and fuse them to the ball. Take the paper off the ball and staight stitch along the curves with brown thread. Add the ball to the cushion, to the left of the bowl.

USE A DOUBLE LENGTH OF THREAD TO STITCH THE MOTIFS TO THE BED; YOU WILL NEED THE EXTRA STRENGTH (AND MAYBE A THIMBLE) WHEN YOU ARE SEWING THROUGH THE THICK FABRIC.

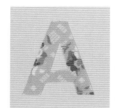

Greeting Cards

Cath Kidston

SKILL RATING: 1

WHAT YOU WILL NEED...

- Selection of greeting-card blanks or sheets of thin Bristol board to make your own cards
- Fusible adhesive web
- Iron and pressing cloth
- Fabric: selection of scraps
- Glue stick
- Tracing paper
- Assortment of paper in different patterns and textures

A handmade card means far more than any store-bought greeting: show your family and friends you care by creating a one-of-a-kind original.

1 To make a fabric design, trace the reversed motifs onto fusible adhesive web, iron them onto fabric scraps, and cut out as for fabric appliqué. If you are using felt, use a pressing cloth.

2 Remove the backing papers and fix the motifs to the card with a glue stick (the heat of an iron would damage the card).

3 To make a paper design, like this colorful flowerpot, use an old-fashioned tracing technique. Draw the reversed outline onto tracing paper. Turn the paper over and rub your pencil, slightly flattened, over the lines.

4 Transfer each shape onto the wrong side of the decorative paper by drawing over the original pencil line once again. Find out the order of assembly for the multilayered designs by turning to the appliqué instructions on pages 18–19: the flowerpot is on page 175.

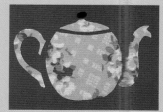

BECOME A MAGPIE AND COLLECT PRETTY POSTCARDS, DIAMANTÉS, SILVER FOIL, WRAPPING PAPER, CANDY WRAPPERS, ODD BUTTONS, RIBBONS, AND OTHER SCRAP MATERIALS TO RECYCLE INTO CARDS.

Stanley Pillow

Cath Kidston

SKILL RATING: 3

WHAT YOU WILL NEED...

- Pillow cover of desired size
- Tracing paper
- Soft leather or suede: 4" x 4³/₄" dark brown; 10" square of light brown; scrap of red
- Glue stick
- Embroidery floss in dark brown, red, and light brown
- Leather sewing needle
- Dressmaker's disappearing-ink pen
- Sewing workbasket (see page 15)

Who could fail to be delighted with this endearing Stanley pillow cover?

1 With a sharp pencil, draw the Stanley outline on page 148 onto tracing paper. Cut out the shapes to make your pattern pieces.

2 Draw around the patterns onto the wrong side of the leather, using the pencil (or a white crayon if it's very dark). Cut the collar from red, the back and right leg markings from dark brown, and the other pieces from light brown. Turn them all right side up.

3 Referring back to the template, draw Stanley's features on the head. Using a leather needle, embroider them in dark brown thread, using small straight stitches (see page 20) to build up the ears, eyes, and nose, and backstitch (see page 21) for the mouth.

4 Remove the pillow form from the pillow cover and reassemble the image on the center front. Fit the pieces together like a jigsaw but leave ¹/₈–¹/₄ inch between them. Attach each one to the cover with a thin layer of adhesive from a glue stick. Place a large book on the cover, to weight the pieces down, and leave until the glue is dry.

5 Again using the leather needle, secure the leather pieces with straight stitches, using matching embroidery floss. Put the pillow form back in the cover.

THIS PILLOW HAS IMPECCABLE ECO-CREDENTIALS: THE LIGHT BROWN LEATHER WAS SALVAGED FROM AN OLD JACKET AND THE DARK BROWN SCRAPS CAME FROM AN WORN-OUT BAG.

AS A VARIATION ON THIS THEME, YOU COULD CUT SEVERAL RECTANGLES OF PAPER AND STITCH THEM INSIDE THE FELT COVER TO MAKE A SPECIAL NOTEBOOK.

Felt-Leaved Needle Book

Cath Kidston

SKILL RATING: 2

WHAT YOU WILL NEED...

- Fusible adhesive web
- Iron and pressing cloth
- Felt: 4³⁄₄" x 7¹⁄₂" pink; 3¹⁄₄" x 4" blue; 4" x 9¹⁄₂" yellow; scraps of red, pink, yellow, and green, for the appliqué
- Sewing thread to match felts
- Embroidery floss in blue, yellow, and light green
- 3 buttons
- Sewing workbasket (see page 15)

This pretty needle case would make a welcome present for the keen stitchers among your family and friends—if you can bring yourself to part with it!

1 Turn to page 168 and trace the three layers of a big flower, two small flowers, four leaves, and two dots onto fusible adhesive web. Cut them out roughly and iron onto the felt scraps, matching the colors opposite. Always remember a pressing cloth when working with felt.

2 Cut each shape around the pencil line. Peel off the papers and arrange the red flower, pink flowers, dots, and leaves in the bottom left corner of the blue felt. Iron in place, then add the pink and yellow layers to the red flower.

3 Now add some embellishment. Work straight stitches (see page 20) around each layer of the red flower, the pink flowers, and the dots, using matching sewing thread. Sew a single straight stitch on each leaf in green embroidery floss. Stitch a button to the center of each flower.

4 To make up the book, place the yellow felt centrally on the pink felt and fold in half lengthwise to make a pink book with yellow pages. Pin the two pieces together, close to the fold.

5 Stitch along the left side of the book, by hand or machine. Pin the blue felt to the front cover, aligning the left edge with the stitching. Straight stitch it in place with tiny—almost invisible—stitches, using blue thread.

6 As a final touch, work a line of blue stitches around three sides of the pink felt and yellow stitches around the blue felt, using embroidery floss.

THREAD SOME OF YOUR NEEDLES WITH LENGTHS OF DIFFERENT COLORED THREADS AND KEEP THEM AT HAND IN YOUR BOOK. THIS WILL SAVE TIME IF YOU NEED TO DO AN INSTANT REPAIR.

IF YOU'RE MAKING THIS FOR YOURSELF,
WHY NOT CONTINUE THE THEME AND
APPLIQUÉ FLOWERS ONTO THE BATH
MAT AND EVEN YOUR BATHROBE?

Washcloth and Towel Set

Cath Kidston

SKILL RATING: 1

WHAT YOU WILL NEED...

- White washcloth and hand towel
- Two 3½" wide strips of white cotton fabric: one 3" longer than the washcloth and the other 3 ' longer than the towel's width
- Fusible adhesive web
- Iron
- Plain cotton fabric: small amount each of light blue, green, and pink
- Sewing thread to match fabrics
- Sewing workbasket (see page 15)

This bathroom set is a luxurious accompaniment to a long, pampering soak, complete with scented soap and fragrant essential oils.

1 The flower motif is on page 172. Enlarge it by 280% to about 1¼ inches, then trace it onto the paper side of fusible adhesive web. Trace six flowers for a 10-inch square washcloth and 12 for a 20-inch wide hand towel—trace more for a larger towel.

2 Cut the flowers out roughly and iron the adhesive side onto the light blue, green, and pink cotton fabrics, making sure you have an equal number of each color. Trim them neatly around the edge and snip out the center holes with short-bladed scissors. Peel off the papers.

3 Leaving a 2-inch space at each end, arrange six flowers along the center of the short fabric strip in a pink-blue-green color sequence. Work straight stitches (see page 20) around each flower, using matching sewing thread.

4 Press under a 1 inch turning along each edge of the decorated fabric strip. Pin the strip centrally to one edge of the washcloth, so that it lies 2 inches from the hem and there is a short overlap at each side. Pin in place, turning the overlap to the back, then slip stitch down with white sewing thread.

5 Decorate the towel in the same way.

LAUNDER THE APPLIQUÉ FABRIC, THE TOWEL, AND WASHCLOTH
IN A HOT WASH BEFORE YOU START WORK; NEW TERRY CLOTH
WILL INEVITABLY SHRINK WHEN FIRST WASHED.

Baby Towel

This hooded baby towel, decorated with the charming songbird motif, makes a useful and pretty gift to welcome a new arrival.

1 You will find the reversed outline of this motif on page 162. Increase the size by 275% so that it fits inside the hood.

2 Following the dotted line, trace the underbody onto fusible adhesive web, then draw the other parts of the bird. Cut out roughly, and then fuse them onto felt: the body to light stone felt, the "cheek" to pink, the breast to red, the beak and foot to dark brown. Always use a pressing cloth when ironing felt.

3 On a cool setting, iron the wing and tail to the back of the fleece. Cut all the shapes out carefully and peel off the backings.

4 Using the pressing cloth, iron the bird's body to the center of the hood. Layer the other parts on top, then fuse the beak and foot to the towel. Work a few straight stitches for the eye (see page 20), using dark brown embroidery floss.

5 Complete the design with the two roses. Trace all the remaining elements onto fusible adhesive web, then cut the flowers from pink, red, light stone, and brown felt, and the leaves and stems from green cotton. Remove the papers.

6 Position the roses on either side of the bird, then add the flower centers and the petals. Tuck the stems and leaves under the edges and iron in place, again using the pressing cloth.

7 Secure each appliqué piece to the background with a round of tiny straight stitches, using matching sewing thread.

Cath Kidston

SKILL RATING: 2

WHAT YOU WILL NEED...

- White hooded baby towel
- Fusible adhesive web
- Iron and pressing cloth
- Felt: 4" x 6" pink; 4" square each of red and light stone; scrap of dark brown
- Fleece: 4" square of dark stone
- Plain cotton fabric: 4" square of green
- Sewing thread to match fabrics
- Embroidery floss in dark brown
- Sewing workbasket (see page 15)

TO PROTECT THE APPLIQUÉ, HAND WASH THE TOWEL IN COLD WATER ONLY WHEN NECESSARY, AND TRY TO AVOID GETTING THE HOOD WET.

FOR AN EVEN MORE COLORFUL
EFFECT, TRY USING PATTERNED
FLEECE OR A DIFFERENT MOTIF.

Starry Fleece Blanket

Cath Kidston

SKILL RATING: 3

WHAT YOU WILL NEED...

- Pink fleece blanket
- Fleece: 32" x 39" red
- Basting thread
- Sewing thread in red
- Sewing workbasket (see page 15)

Teddies and toddlers alike will want to cozy up under this warm, lightweight blanket.

1 The outline templates for this project are on page 154. To make the paper patterns, pick out four or five different stars and enlarge them by 200%. Cut out the photocopied stars around the outline.

2 Pin the patterns to the right side of the fleece and cut them out. My blanket measured 32 inches by 39 inches and is covered with 45 evenly spaced stars—you will need to make more for a larger blanket or fewer for a smaller one.

3 Arrange the stars across the blanket, balancing the arrangement of size and shape. Pin them in place when you are pleased with the composition, then baste down close to the edge.

4 Sew the stars to the blanket by working a round of straight stitches around the outside edge of each one (see page 20), using matching red sewing thread. Remove the basting.

FLEECE FABRIC SHOULD NOT BE IRONED, SO A TRADITIONAL METHOD OF HAND-STITCHED APPLIQUÉ IS USED HERE TO SECURE THE STARS TO THE FLUFFY BLANKET.

GAUNTLET GLOVES LIKE THESE
HAVE A DEEP, PLAIN CUFF.
IF YOU CAN'T FIND ANY,
EMBROIDER THE DESIGN ONTO
THE BACK OF THE HAND.

Rose Gloves

Cath Kidston

SKILL RATING: 3

WHAT YOU WILL NEED...

- Pair of cashmere gloves
- Lightweight nonwoven iron-on interfacing
- Dressmaker's disappearing-ink pen
- Iron and pressing cloth
- Embroidery floss in pink, red, antique white, dark brown, and green
- Sewing workbasket (see page 15)

Keep your fingers toasty warm on the coldest day with these embroidered gloves. The rose detail makes them completely unique.

1 Photocopy the single rose outline on the right of page 162 at 115%, then make a second, reversed enlargement. Lay a piece of interfacing over the first motif with the smooth (nonadhesive) side facing upward. Using a disappearing-ink pen, draw over the lines.

2 Trim the motif around the outside edge. Fuse the iron-on interfacing to the center of the cuff (or the back of the hand) with a cool iron and a pressing cloth.

3 Using embroidery floss, fill in each area with satin stitch (see page 20). Start with the pink petals, then the red and antique white. Finish the rose with a dark brown center. Work the leaves in green, slanting the stitches on each side toward the center.

4 Embroider the other rose onto the second glove in the same way, so that you have a matching pair.

IF YOU ENJOY STITCHING ON KNITWEAR, YOU COULD MAKE A COMPLETE WINTER ACCESSORY SET. WORK A SINGLE MOTIF ON EACH GARMENT OR SCATTER SEVERAL ACROSS A BERET OR ALONG A MATCHING SCARF.

Be
Inspired

It was very difficult to decide which projects to include in the book, as each design would work equally well on so many different items. Whether it's the sailing-boat on a T-shirt, pillow, or bag, or the strawberries along the edge of a bed sheet, dishtowel or skirt, the variations are endless. Over the next few pages I have laid out some more ideas for you, but half the fun will be choosing for yourself what to customize and how, using the techniques you have learned.

Be Inspired

T-shirt

T-shirts are one of the least expensive and easiest items to adapt. Why not initial T-shirts and give them away as personalized gifts? Remember, you don't only have to work on the front; think about decorating the sleeves and the back of the t-shirt as well.

Beret

If you liked the beret on page 90, you could customize a wool hat in the same way—great for a ski holiday! You could also embroider a simple design onto the hat—perhaps one of the rose motifs to give a prettier, more delicate look to the beret.

Skirt

Plain appliqué would work well on a patterned skirt, as it will contrast with the background design. Or you could layer on other prints for a great "patchwork" effect. You could just decorate around the hem if covering the whole skirt is a little daunting.

Tote Bag

You can pick up inexpensive eco bags all over the place, and they are ideal for working on as they are such a simple shape. Consider embroidering over simple appliqué designs to create a textured, layered effect. You could also add a handy pocket inside, as shown on the strawberry apron on page 32. So that the stitching isn't visible on the outside, first make a simple lining and attach the pocket to that.

Apron

You could add one larger pocket to your apron using the same technique outlined on page 32. The breakfast template would work well here—maybe a row of boiled eggs or cups and saucers along the bottom? Or for a simpler project, why not cover the whole apron in colorful dots?

Sweater

There's now no need to throw out a much-loved, but tired old sweater. You can easily disguise moth holes and worn elbows using scraps of patterned fabric. Or you could embroider a simple motif onto the front in place of the initials on page 80.

Socks

As well as embroidering onto bed socks, what about thick walking socks or giving a pair of personalized baby booties as a gift? The embroidery method used on page 50 would also work well added to a sweater as a single motif.

Purse

Why not decorate a purse and use it as "wrapping" for a precious present like a piece of jewelry? You could cover the whole purse in embroidery, or keep it simple with a single design on the back. Maybe you could match your purse to one of the designs in the bags chapter, or make a shawl or scarf using the same template.

Scarf

If you liked our racing car scarf on page 86, why not try another design? You could appliqué circles or flowers all the way up it? Or you could spell out your favorite team name to make your own soccer scarf! Jersey fabric is inexpensive and doesn't fray—fantastic for an instant scarf!

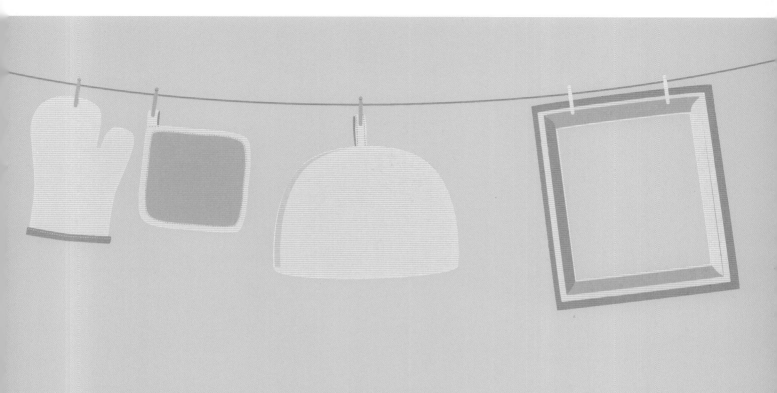

Oven Mitt and Pot Holder

Why not take the colors of your own home as the palette for your kitchen accessories to make a really chic look? You could make some matching dishtowels (see page 26) and an apron (see page 32). Any of the templates would work with these items—you could have a very simple spotty theme running throughout the kitchen.

Teapot Cozy

You can easily make a teapot cozy by cutting up an old blanket and blanket-stitching around the curved edges. You could use the cup and saucer template to great effect here. If you're feeling ambitious, the country cottage would be a more traditional design to use (see page 56).

Picture Frame

A dusty old frame can quickly be transformed with a lick of glossy paint. Think about making a set of pictures by using different sections of the same template, or the same template completed in contrasting colors.

Addresses

Embroidery floss

For 6-strand cotton embroidery floss, look in your local craft or fabric stores, which will usually stock a wide range of colors.

For the DMC cotton embroidery floss used in this book, go to the following websites:

DMC
www.dmc-usa.com
Visit the DMC website to find a store near you that carries DMC products. When you first enter the website, look for the "Store Locator" and click on this. Just enter your zip code and your nearest stores will pop up.

Herrschners
herrschners.com
This online store carries all the DMC products and the full range of 6-strand DMC embroidery floss colors. When you enter the site, select "Shop by Brand" and click on "DMC." Alternatively, go directly to the cotton embroidery floss by typing in the following:
http://herrschners.com/Product/6Strand+DMC+Embroidery+Floss.aspx

Fabrics

The fabrics used in this book for appliqué are mainly solid-colored cottons and felt, and some cotton prints. Tweeds, plastic-coated fabric, and fleece are also used for a few projects.

If possible, find your fabrics at a local fabric store, where you will be able to buy small remnants. Another option is to use fabrics from recycled clothing (see page 140).

You can also try the following websites to locate your nearest fabric stores or to shop online. To help you in your search, the sites are divided into general fabrics (and notions), quilting fabrics, luxury quilting fabrics, and felts.

For other cotton fabric sources online, you will get the best results by searching for "quilting fabrics."

GENERAL FABRICS AND NOTIONS
Try these sites for general fabrics, iron-on interfacing (for embroidered motifs), fusible adhesive web (for appliqué), sewing threads, tools, and notions:

Fabric Depot
www.fabricdepot.com

Fabric.com
www.fabric.com

Jo-Ann fabric and craft stores
www.joann.com
Go to the website to use the store locator to find a Jo-Ann near you. Jo-Ann is also good for fusible adhesive web, iron-on interfacing, marking pens, sewing threads, and sewing tools.

Hancock Fabrics
www.hancockfabrics.com

Mood Fabrics
www.moodfabrics.com
Sell online but also have a 40,000-square-foot mega store on 37th Street in Manhattan. They say, "If you can't find the fabric at Mood, it doesn't exist."

QUILTING FABRICS
These sources are good for cotton fabrics—both prints and solids

Born to Quilt
www.borntoquilt.com

eQuilter
www.equilter.com

Fabric Blowout
www.fabricblowout.com

Fat Quarter Shop
www.fatquartershop.com

Hayloft Fabrics
www.hayloftfabrics.com

LUXURY QUILTING FABRICS
If you are looking for something a little special, try the Cath Kidston website for fabrics (see page 141) or visit the following websites. All these sites offer high-quality, designer-led quilting fabrics:

Cia's Palette
www.ciaspalette.com
High-quality 100% cottons.

Free Spirit Fine Quilting Fabric
www.freespiritfabric.com
Designer fabrics.

Reprodepot Fabrics
www.reprodepotfabrics.com
Started in 1999 with vintage textiles, this site now offers new fabrics with vintage and retro themes.

Felt

As explained on page 15, the best felt to use for felt appliqué is 100% wool felt. The felt in craft stores is usually the synthetic variety, so it may be easier to find your wool felt online. The sites listed here sell all-wool felts and/or wool-blend felts (usually blends of wool and rayon). You can buy their felts in small sheets of various sizes and sometimes by the yard.

A Child's Dream Come True
www.achildsdream.com
Have Holland 100% wool felt in 61 colors. Also sell plant-dyed felt in 15 lovely colors.

Colonial Crafts
www.colonialcrafts.com
Sell National Nonwovens 100% wool felt in small sheets of various sizes.

Erica's Craft & Sewing Center
www.ericas.com
Have 100% wool and wool-blend felts. Also available on the site are good care instructions for wool felt, so worth the visit for that alone.

Felt-o-rama
www.feltorama.com
Excellent source of 100% wool German felt and wool-blend felt in small sheets and by the yard. Good for hard-to-find colors and quality felts.

Joggles
www.joggles.com
Everything for the textile, cloth doll, and mixed media artist. Sell assorted odds and ends of National Nonwoven felts in a one-pound bundle.

Magic Cabin
www.magiccabin.com
Sell hig-quallity, medium-weight 100% wool felt in many colors. Available in 56-color pack of 9-inch-by-12-inch sheets, or in individual 18-inch squares.

Weir Dolls & Crafts
www.weirdollsandcrafts.com
Have soft medium-weight 100% wool felt from Nepal. Comes in 47 colors.

Wool Felt Central
www.prairiepointjunction.com
This site offers wool-blend felts as well as a selection of colors of DMC floss.

Vintage Clothing Stores

Instead of buying new clothes to decorate for some of the projects in this book, you can always recycle old clothes from vintage clothing stores. Aside from garage sales, here are few sources:

Ballyhoo Vintage
www.ballyhoovintage.com

eBay
www.ebay.com
A great place to find vintage clothes.

Monster Vintage
www.monstervintage.com

Posh Girl Vintage
www.poshgirlvintage.com

Rusty Zipper
www.rustyzipper.com

Cheap Jack's
www.cheapjacks.com

Dandelion Vintage
www.dandelionvintage.com

Flea Markets and Antiques Fairs

Flea markets and antiques fairs are good places to find old frames, sheets, curtains, tablecloths, place mats, and pillowcases for some of the projects in this book. You will be able to find local flea markets and antiques fairs online (see Collector.org), but here are a few to get you started.

Allegan Antiques Market
www.alleganantiques.com
Allegan, Michigan.

Annex/Hell's Kitchen Flea Market
www.hellskitchenfleamarket.com
New York City.

Antique and Collectible Market
www.zurkpromotions.com/Grayslake
Grayslake, Illinois.

Antiques by the Bay
www.antiquesbybay.com
Almeda, California.

Austin Country Flea Market
www.austincountry.citymax.com

Brimfield Antiques Show
www.brimfield.com
Three times a year in Brimfield, Massachusetts with 6,000 vendors.

Collectors.org
collectors.org
The home of collecting on the internet. Has a US flea market directory.

Daytona Flea and Farmers Market
www.daytonafleamarket.com
One of the top flea markets in the US.

Kane County Flea Market
www.kanecountyfleamarket.com
St. Charles, Illinois.

Rhinebeck Antiques Fair
www.rhinebeckantiquesfair.com
Rhinebeck, New York.

Rose Bowl Flea Market
www.rgcshows.com/RoseBowlFleaMarket
World-famous flea market in Pasadena, California.

Scott Antique Market
www.scottantiquemarket.com
Atlanta, Georgia and Columbus, Ohio.

Cath Kidston products

Cath Kidston designs can be obtained from stores in the UK, Ireland, and Japan, and online at:

www.cathkidston.co.uk

Visit the website to see the wide range of Cath Kidston products. They include women's and children's clothing, as well as accessories, such as bags, badges, hankies, jewelry, key rings, purses, and wallets. You will also find a big selection of homeware, such as fabric, cushions, sewing baskets, sewing kits, knitting-needle cases, tablecloths, tin canisters, and much more.

If you do not want to shop online and are planning a visit to the UK or Ireland, search the store locator on the website to find a store near your destination selling Cath Kidston products. Only the London shops are listed here.

Cath Kidston's stores in London

London (Chelsea)
12 Cale Street
London
SW3 3QU
020 7584 3232

London (Chiswick)
125 Chiswick High Road
London
W4 2ED
020 8995 8052

London (Covent Garden)
28–32 Shelton Street
London
WC2H 9JE
020 7836 4803

London (Fulham)
668 Fulham Road
London
SW6 5RX
020 7731 6531

London (Holland Park)
8 Clarendon Cross
London
W11 4AP
020 7221 4000

London (Kings Road)
322 Kings Road
London
SW3 5UH
020 7351 7335

London (Knightsbridge)
Concession in **Harvey Nichols**, Knightsbridge, London

London (Marylebone)
51 Marylebone High Street
London
W1U 5HW
020 7935 6555

Acknowledgments

Many thanks to Jess Pemberton for making all of the projects, Pia Tryde, Karina Mamrowicz, Jenny Walker, Laura Mackay, Jo Sanders, Bridget Bodoano, Elaine Ashton, and Lucinda Ganderton. Thanks also to Katherine Case, Laura Herring, Anne Furniss, and Helen Lewis at Quadrille. This book is dedicated to Stanley.

Editorial Director: Anne Furniss
Art Director: Helen Lewis
Project Editor: Laura Herring
Designer: Katherine Case
Photographer: Pia Tryde
Illustrations: Bridget Bodoano, Laura Mackay
Project Designer and Maker: Jessica Pemberton
Needlework Consultant: Lucinda Ganderton
Pattern Checker: Sally Harding
Production Director: Vincent Smith
Production Controller: Ruth Deary

For information, address St. Martin's Press, 175 Fifth Avenue, New York, N.Y. 10010.

www.stmartins.com

The written instructions, photographs, designs, patterns, and projects in this volume are intended for personal use of the reader and may be reproduced for that purpose only.

Library of Congress Cataloging-in-Publication Data Available Upon Request

ISBN-13: 978-0-312-59686-6

First Edition: January 2010

10 9 8 7 6 5 4 3 2 1

Templates

Racing Car 145–146

Stanley 147–148

Cowboy 149–150

Sailboat 151–152

Stars 153–154

Bubbles 155–156

Flowers 157–158

Alphabet 159–160

ABCDE
FGHIJK
LMNOP
QRSTU
VWXYZ

Songbird 161–162

Antique Rose 163–164

Basket of Flowers 165–166

Circus Flowers 167–168

Strawberry 169–170

Breakfast 171–172

Country Cottage 173–174

Flowerpot 175–176

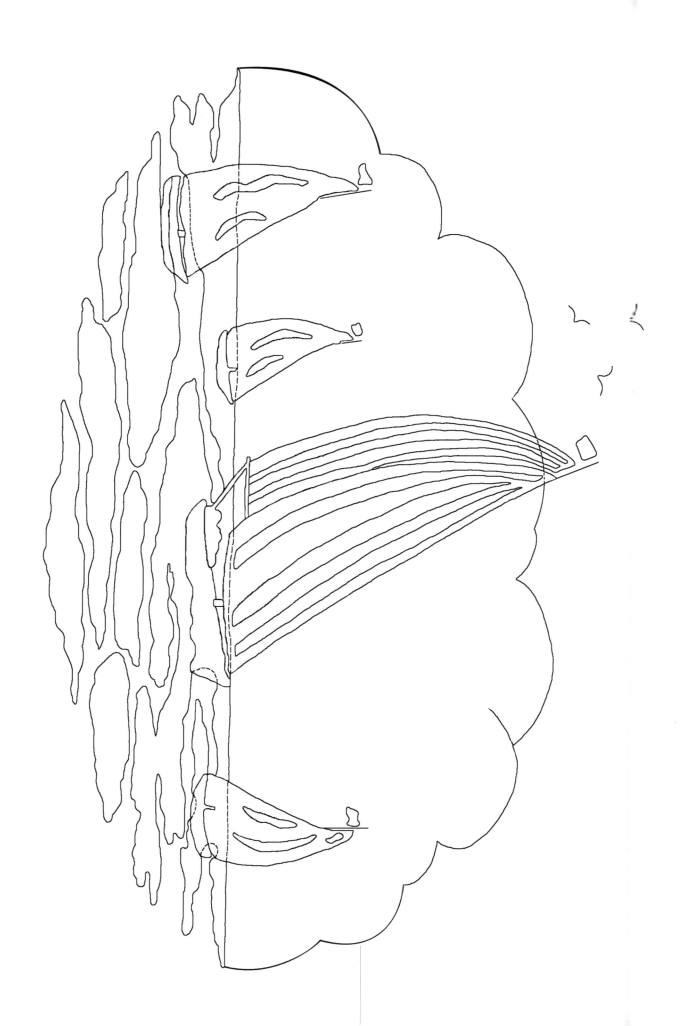

ABCDE
FGHIJK
LMNOP
QRSTU
VWXYZ

ABCDE

FGHIJK

LMNOP

QRSTU

VWXYZ